The Two Lives of
Flora MacDonald

The Two Lives of Flora MacDonald

The Life of Flora Macdonald, and Her Adventures with Prince Charles

Alexander Macgregor

Flora Macdonald in America

J. P. Maclean

With a Copy of the Declaration of Miss MacDonald, Apple Cross Bay, July 12th 1746

LEONAUR

The Two Lives of Flora MacDonald
The Life of Flora Macdonald, and Her Adventures with Prince Charles
by Alexander Macgregor
Flora Macdonald in America
by J. P. Maclean
With a Copy of the Declaration of Miss MacDonald Apple Cross Bay, July 12th
1746

FIRST EDITION

First published under the titles
The Life of Flora Macdonald, and Her Adventures with Prince Charles
and
Flora Macdonald in America

Leonaur is an imprint of Oakpast Ltd

Copyright in this form © 2016 Oakpast Ltd

ISBN: 978-1-78282-537-1 (hardcover)
ISBN: 978-1-78282-538-8 (softcover)

http://www.leonaur.com

Contents

The Life of Flora Macdonald, and Her Adventures with Prince Charles

Contents

CHAPTER 1

From Sheriffmuir to Culloden

The various circumstances connected with the Rebellions of 1715 and 1745 are minutely recorded in the history of our country. James the Sixth of Scotland and First of England, was the common progenitor of the two families which so long and fiercely contended for the throne of Great Britain. That monarch was succeeded in 1625 by Charles I. who was beheaded twenty-four years after. His son, Charles II., after the death of Cromwell, was placed on the British throne, in the year 1660. Having died without issue, his brother, the Duke of York, under the title of James II. succeeded him in 1685. His reign, however, was but short. He was dethroned four years after on account of his religion, and was compelled to leave the kingdom. His daughter Mary, with William, grandson of Charles I. then succeeded to the throne.

After them, Queen Anne, another daughter of James II. began to reign. She died without issue in the year 1714, leaving behind her a brother named James. This James, being of course the son of James II. is well known in our national history as the pretender, or the Chevalier St. George. He had naturally a keen eye to the kingdom, and was strongly supported in his views to this end by several powerful friends. Among those most devoted to his cause was the Earl of Mar, who had forces of considerable strength in readiness for action. Possessed himself of no small number of willing retainers, he had the benefit of numerous allies from France. James, with no doubt of success, unfurled his banner at Braemar, in the Highlands of Aberdeenshire, in 1715, but notwithstanding all his careful preparations, he was defeated soon after at Sheriffmuir.

Like his father, James II., he was banished from the kingdom, and his various schemes fell to the ground. Amid all these bloody insurrections, the Parliament of the nation bestowed the crown on the nearest Protestant heir, George, Elector of Hanover, and great-grandson of James I. This monarch, styled George I. died in 1727, and was succeeded by his son, George II. In the meantime, James, the Chevalier St. George, had married Clementina, granddaughter of John Sobieski, the heroic King of Poland, by whom he had a son, Charles Edward, born in 1720, who eventually became the hero of the Rebellion of 1745. The *chevalier* had also another son, known in history as the Cardinal de York.

The Chevalier St. George is said to have been a man of little judgment, and of weak and vacillating character, to which may be attributed the failure of his attempt to regain the throne of his ancestors in 1715. But, on the other hand, the blood of Sobieski seems to have invigorated his son, Charles Edward, with greater mental powers, and to have inspired him with that courage, which in 1745-6, during his various campaigns, almost enabled him to retrieve the fortunes of his family.

After the defeat and ruin of the Chevalier St. George in 1715, he escaped, and fled to France, where he lived in seclusion on the bounty of such friends and adherents as continued to sympathise with him. He made no farther attempts to regain the sovereignty which his ancestors possessed, and to which he was, no doubt, legally entitled by the principles of genealogy. Far different, however, was the conduct of his elder son, Prince Charles Edward, although even he, on various occasions, betrayed a lack of prudence and judgment, which was anything but favourable to his cause. To regain the crown of his ancestors was naturally the dream of his youth, and became the daring and romantic effort of his early manhood.

The disappointment of his father, and the abortive issue of the various schemes resorted to by his father's friends, must have awakened him to a sense of the position in which he stood. These things must have had a rousing and inspiring effect upon his sensitive nature, when he had attained to the age of taking cognisance of them, and when, no doubt, his ambition for the British crown must have been mightily intensified by the unexpected fruitlessness of his father's efforts.

Thus influenced and excited, he manifested a firm determination to make the bold attempt, and to embark, perhaps prematurely, on his dangerous enterprise. Consequently, in the twenty-fifth year of his age, he landed in the Highlands of Scotland, utterly unprepared for his hazardous adventure. And how could he have been otherwise, as he there stood without men or money, or the multifarious and necessary munitions of war? There he appeared, and, but to a very few, very unexpectedly—no doubt a very highly prepossessing youth, amiable, affable, and active; but in a lonely, sequestered corner of the West Highlands—in the midst of strangers, with only seven attendants—for the ambitious purpose of regaining the Crown of Great Britain, already possessed by a near relative; and which had been lost to his own family for fifty-seven years! To the wise, this hasty enterprise could hardly fail to appear as a forlorn hope,—yet the youthful prince was sanguine in the extreme. He relied implicitly on the justice of his cause, and not less so on the fidelity and valour of the Highland chiefs and their gallant vassals.

By his amiable manners and captivating address he very soon enlisted the feelings and services of the majority of the Highland clans. The intelligence of his arrival spread with the telegraphy of the "fiery-cross" over mountain and glen. The Highlanders were on the alert, and became speedily aroused. Under the guardianship of their brave chiefs they soon hied to the general rendezvous, where a halo of glory seemed to overshadow their arms, and a confidence of success to inspire their hearts!

The youthful prince placed himself at the head of no insignificant body, and displayed that magnanimity of soul which might be expected in the descendant of Bruce and Sobieski! His soldiers were, no doubt, untrained, and unskilled in the more scientific modes of carrying on a great war, but they possessed all the qualities which go to make good soldiers; their valour and endurance were great. It is well known that with these untutored but devoted followers, the prince took possession of Scotland, penetrated England as far as Derby, and caused His Majesty, King George II. to tremble on his throne! Had he boldly entered London, as he had done our Scottish towns, it is difficult to say what the result might have been; but for various causes he determined to retreat to the Highlands for the winter, rather than advance on the Capital of the British Empire, although he was within a hundred miles of it.

From that moment the prospects of the prince began to look gloomy. His bright star began to wane, until on the 16th of April, 1746, it was completely extinguished on the bloody moor of Culloden! On that ill-selected field his army was broken to pieces by the well-trained forces of the Duke of Cumberland. His brave Highlanders fell in hundreds by his side, and he himself became a fugitive and outlaw in the land of his Royal ancestors. Escaping from the scene of slaughter and defeat, he withdrew, with all possible speed, to the western parts of the county of Inverness, in the hope of effecting his escape by sea to France. In this, he was, however, for a time unsuccessful.

At Moyhall, the residence of the Mackintosh of Mackintosh, within twelve miles of Inverness, the prince had a very narrow escape from falling into the hands of the enemy. The chief of Mackintosh himself was loyal to the government, and was greatly guided in his movements by his neighbour, President Forbes of Culloden. Lady Mackintosh, on the other hand, like many others of her sex, was warmly favourable to the pretentions of the prince. By her influence she privately induced many of her clan to support his cause. At that time, as related by Cameron in his *Traditions of Skye:*

> The Earl of Loudon was at Inverness with nearly 2000 men, and he resolved to secure the prince as prisoner before he could be joined by his army, which was marching from the south. The earl advanced towards Moy with 1500 men, the advance guard of 70 men being commanded by Macleod of Macleod. Lady Mackintosh received private information of the contemplated attack, and sent the prince to a place of safety. In the meantime, she sent out a patrolling party of five men armed with muskets to watch the road from Inverness, of whom the blacksmith, a clever fellow of the name of Fraser, assumed the command.
>
> On the approach of the Earl of Loudon's army, during the night of the 16th of February, 1746, the smith placed his men at intervals along the roadside, and ordered them to fire at the head of the advancing column, raising a shout, and calling on the "Camerons" and "Macdonalds" to advance—thus leading Loudon's men to believe that they were confronted by a large body of the prince's army! Donald Bàn MacCrimmon, Macleod of Macleod's piper, was killed by the blacksmith's shot, close by Macleod's side. Loudon's men, thinking they had to contend against a superior force, made a hasty retreat to Inverness; known in history as the "Rout of Moy." The poor piper was the only person killed, and the Macleods carried his body to Inverness.

Donald Bàn MacCrimmon was reputed the best piper of his day in the Highlands. When leaving Dunvegan, he had a presentiment that he would never return from this expedition, and he composed on that occasion that plaintive air, "Cha Till mi Tuilleadh," or "Mac-Crimmon's Lament," which he played on his pipes as the independent companies of the Macleods were leaving Dunvegan, while their wives and sweethearts were waving them a sorrowful farewell. To this air MacCrimmon composed a feeling Gaelic song, the sentiments of which are well brought out in the English imitation by Sir Walter Scott, as follows:—

Macleod's wizard flag from the grey castle sallies,
The rowers are seated, unmoored are the galleys;
Gleam war-axe and broadsword, clang target and quiver,
As MacCrimmon plays "Farewell to Dunvegan for ever".

Farewell to each cliff, on which breakers are foaming,
Farewell each dark glen in which red deer are roaming,
Farewell lonely Skye, to lake, mountain, and river,
Macleod may return, but MacCrimmon shall never.

Farewell the bright clouds that on Cullin are sleeping;
Farewell the bright eyes in the Fort that are weeping;
To each minstrel delusion farewell! and for ever—
MacCrimmon departs to return to you never!

The Banshee's wild voice sings the death dirge before me,
And the pall of the dead for a mantle hangs o'er me;
But my heart shall not fly, and my nerve shall not quiver,
Tho' devoted I go—to return again never!

Too oft shall the note of MacCrimmon bewailing
Be heard when the Gael on their exile are sailing;
Dear land! to the shores whence unwilling we sever,
Return, return, return, we shall never!

A female bard at Dunvegan, on hearing MacCrimmon's Lament played, is said to have composed the following beautiful response:—

Dh' iadh ceo 'nan stuc mu aodann Chuilinn,
'Us sheinn a' bhean-shith a torman mulaid,
Tha suilean gorm ciuin 'san Dun a' sileadh,
O'n thriall thu bh' uainn, 's nach till thu tuilleadh.

Cha till, cha till, cha till MacCruimein
A'n cogadh no sith, cha till e tuilleadh,
Le airgiod no ni cha till MacCruimein,
Cha till gu brath, gu la na cruinne.

Tha osag nan gleann gu fann ag imeachd;
Gach sruthan 's gach allt gu mall le bruthaich;
Tha ialt' nan speur feadh gheugan dubhach,
A' caoidh gu'n d' thalbh 's nach till thu tuilleadh.
        Cha till, cha till, &c.

Tha'n fhairge fadheoidh lan broin 'us mulaid,
Tha'm bata fo sheol, ach dhiult i siubhal;
Tha gair nan tonn le fuaim neo-shubhach,
Ag radh gu'n d' fhalbh 's nach till thu tuilleadh.
        Cha till, cha till, &c.

Cha chluinnear do cheol 'san Dun mu fheasgar,
'S mac-talla nam mur le muirn 'ga fhreagairt;
Gach fleasgach 'us aigh, gu'n cheol, gu'n bheadradh,
O'n thriall thu bh' uainn, 's nach till thu tuilleadh.
Cha till, cha till, cha till MacCruimein,
A'n cogadh no sith, cha till e tuilleadh,
Le airgiod no ni cha till MacCruimein,
Cha till gu brath, gu la na cruinne.

The MacCrimmons were for ages the distinguished pipers of the Macleods of Dunvegan, and in consequence had a free gift of the extensive farm called Borevaig, which they enjoyed for many generations from sire to son. The Macdonalds of the Isles had likewise their own race of pipers—the MacArthurs, to whom was granted a perpetual gift of the farm of Peingowen, near the castle of Duntulm. Great rivalry existed between the two races of pipers, as each strove for the superiority. Both the MacCrimmons and the MacArthurs noted down their *piobaireachds* by a sort of syllabic vocables, somewhat like the Sol-fa system of noting music; and by this process they preserved their tunes, and could play them off at pleasure. They made large collections of their *piobaireachds* in this way, and tradition says that Donald Bàn, who was killed at the Rout of Moy, excelled most of his race by the beauty and neatness with which he noted the salutes and laments, which he composed and played so exquisitely.

The field of Battle of Culloden, immediately after the desperate struggle, presented a dismal appearance. The bodies of the slain Highlanders lay in heaps upon the gory plain. These brave sons of the mountains and glens fell with their faces to the foe, after displaying, under every disadvantage, an amount of stern heroism peculiar to themselves. No power on their part could have withstood the artillery and cavalry of the enemy, as to them, every circumstance of time and place was adverse as foot-soldiers, while to Cumberland's trained forces all was favourable. The events of the day were sadly mismanaged for the cause of the prince, and although the Highlanders fought with their usual bravery, they were unable to overcome impossibilities.

The following *stanzas* by T. D. Fraser, Melbourne, graphically delineate the harrowing scenes of—

CULLODEN.

Wild waves the heath on Culloden's bleak moor,
As it waved on that morn long ago—
When warriors proud on its bosom it bore,
That trembled and shook with the Camerons' loud roar,
And the shouts of each terrible foe.

Oh! ill-fated Stuart, the last of thy race,
Though nobly thy right thou didst claim—
The tear starts unbidden, when round us we trace
The scene of thy ruin, unstained by disgrace,
Thy conquest untainted by shame.

And ye gallant spirits, the brave and the true,
Who stained the brown heath with the gore
That followed each terrible stroke that ye drew—
Alas! that your own should have mingled there too,
And your names pass from earth evermore.

Oh! proudly and high waved your plumes as ye passed,
And high throbbed your hearts to the sound
Of the war-pipe that breathed out its soul-stirring blast,
That to the firm onslaught hurried ye fast—
And alas! to a hero's red mound.

Like leaves by the tempest all scattered abroad,
So here were ye scattered around,
And here were ye piled high on the red sward,
Still grasping in death each deeply dyed sword
That had reddened the cold murky ground.

And when through your ranks like an angel of death,
Poured the fierce storm of iron hail,
That levelled your bravest all low as the heath
As the forest leaves strewn by the whirlwind's wild breath,
Even then your stout hearts did not quail!

"To the charge, to the charge," was your answering cry,
"Lead us on, lead us on, 'gainst the foe,
Why stand we inactive thus tamely to die?"
All powerless to fight, and disdaining to fly—
To the charge, to the charge!—weal or woe.

Ah! ne'er in all time, shall that charge be forgot,
Inscribed on the annals of fame;
Your souls passed away all undimmed by one blot
Of one selfish thought from that blood-reeking spot,
Which still is enbalmed with your name.

Flora mcdonald

CHAPTER 2

From Culloden to the Long Island

Notwithstanding the favourable issue of the Battle of Culloden to the Royal forces, there was still a dread that hostilities might eventually be, in some shape, renewed by the Highlanders. To counteract this as much as possible, very stern measures were resorted to. The government, sensible of the dangerous nature of the prince's claims, and of the number and power of his friends in Scotland, immediately resolved to set the high price of £30,000 upon his head! Such a sum in those days was enormous wealth, especially in the eyes of a poor Highlander, and would be no insignificant fortune even in the present; yet to the immortal honour of the Highlanders, not one was found sufficiently mean to betray his prince, or sufficiently covetous to take this large and tempting reward of blood.

With all our advancement in civilisation in the present day—with all the advantages of the schoolmaster abroad—and with all cur religious attainments, it is questionable, indeed, if the same munificent bribe were offered under similar circumstances today, (1882), whether it would be attended with the same honourable result.

Having thus briefly alluded to a few genealogical and historical incidents in the eventful career of the unfortunate prince, a rapid sketch of his many hair-breadth escapes, and severe deprivations previous to his rescue from the Long Island, by the gallantry of the young lady whose early life will form the chief subject of the following pages, may prove interesting.

Charles, deeply chagrined by the sad, and, to him, unexpected result of the battle, lost no time in setting off for a place of safety. He hastily assembled some of his more steadfast adherents, and entreated them to accompany him as quickly as possible from the scene of danger. Accordingly, he left the field. Having provided a considerable body of horse, as well as several foot soldiers, he departed along with Sir Thomas Sheridan, Captain O'Neal, Mr. John Hay, Mr. O'Sullivan, a faithful old Highlander named Edward Burke, who acted as guide, and several others.

They crossed the River Nairn at the farmhouse of Faillie, between three and four miles from Culloden, by one of General Wade's bridges. Here the prince halted to consult his friends as to what was best to be done. The Highland chiefs engaged in the insurrection did not as yet despair, but still expected that they might be able to rally, and eventually succeed in gaining the great object in view. It was, however, apparent that the prince did not at heart sympathise with the plans of those who had already sacrificed so much for his cause. Chambers says:

> His wish was to make his way as quickly as possible to France, in order to use personal exertions in procuring those powerful supplies which had been so much and so vainly wished for. He expected to find French vessels hovering on the West Coast, in one of which he might obtain a quick passage to that country. He had therefore determined to proceed in this direction without loss of time.

Meantime it was agreed that the horse and the greater part of his attendants should part with the prince at the bridge of Faillie, which was done. The gentlemen present, no doubt, with the concurrence of several other absent adherents, resolved, contrary to the inclination of His Royal Highness, to meet as soon as possible at Ruthven in Badenoch, in order, if practicable, to prosecute the cause anew. After bidding farewell to his faithful friends, he set off for Stratherrick, accompanied by Sheridan, O'Sullivan, O'Neal, and one or two others, guided forward by Burke, who was well acquainted with the route.

The country was deplorably desolated. Dwelling-houses and cottages were deserted by their inmates, who had fled to the rocks and mountains for shelter from the reputed cruelty of the enemy. The whole scene seemed to have been visited by the gloom of death! Meanwhile the party, crushed with fatigue and hunger, arrived at the steading of Tordarroch, but found the dwelling shut up, and no living soul near it. They then wandered on to Aberarder, and there found matters to be the same. From Aberarder they moved along to Farraline House, where they fared no better. At length with much ado, they reached Gorthlig House, the residence of Mr. Thomas Fraser, then acting as manager and factor for Lord Lovat.

It happened at this time that Simon, Lord Lovat, resided at his factor's house, and very likely made a point of being present on that memorable day, as by his instructions, a great feast was in the way of being prepared to celebrate the expected victory of the prince that afternoon on the moor of Culloden. How crestfallen Lovat must have been when the prince had hastily revealed to him the sad tidings of the day, and the irretrievable ruin of his person, his prospects, and his family, may be easily imagined! Various accounts are given of the effects the intelligence produced on the aged chief. It is said that he became frantic with alarm, and fled to the field beyond the dwelling, exclaiming, "Cut off my head at once! Chop it off; chop it off!" By another account, he is represented as having "received the prince with expressions of attachment, but reproached him severely for his intention of abandoning the enterprise," (*vide* Chambers' *History of the Rebellion of* 1745-6, also Burke's *Narrative. Jacobite Memoirs*).

The prince having thus passed a few hours in conversation with his lordship, it was deemed utterly unsafe that he should remain there during the night, so, after liberally partaking of the excellent viands laid before them, which they stood so much in need of, the prince and his friends bade farewell to old Simon, and set off across the hill to Fort Augustus, where they made no stay, but pushed on to Invergarry, the romantic stronghold of Macdonald of Glengarry. There they arrived a little before sunrise, and found everything wearing a most cheerless aspect. The great halls of the castle, which often resounded with the shrill notes of the *piobaireachd*, and lavished their hospitality on high and low, were on that morning desolate and empty.

The castle had been completely dismantled, the furniture removed, the walls made bare, and the whole fabric appeared the emblem of desolation and ruin! One solitary individual was found in this once lordly mansion, but he had nothing to give to the weary wanderers to refresh them, but some fish to eat, and the hard, cold floor for a bed. They all slept, however, for several hours in their clothes, but on awaking from their unrefreshing repose, the whole party deemed it prudent to take leave of the prince, with the exception of O'Neal, O'Sullivan, and Edward Burke. His Royal Highness at this place received a long communication from Lord George Murray, dated Ruthven, recapitulating the numerous blunders that had been committed, and stating that various chiefs, with an army of between two and three thousand men, had assembled at Ruthven, ready to commence the campaign anew, on their receiving the commands of His Royal Highness to do so. The prince sent back a message requesting the army immediately to disperse. The chronicler says:

> In thus resigning the contest, which, by his inconsiderate rashness, he had provoked, Charles showed that he was not possessed of that magnanimity which many of his followers ascribed to him.

On the evening of the same day Prince Charles and his small party left Glengarry's inhospitable mansion, and betook themselves to Loch Arkaig, in the country of the Camerons. They arrived late at night at Clunes, where everything possible was done for their comfort. Old Cameron of Clunes had been an officer in Lochiel's regiment, and was killed at Prestonpans, fighting bravely for his prince. His son and heir, Young Clunes, felt much for the misfortunes that lately befell the prince's cause, and, pitying his forlorn condition, devised a plan for his safety. A secure and suitable cave was fitted up comfortably for the use of His Royal Highness and his friends. Provisions were furnished for the occasion, and to entertain the party well, Clunes killed an ox, ordered a portion of it to be immediately dressed and carried to the cave where the fugitives were concealed.

Besides all this, a substantial supply of bread, cheese, and whisky was forwarded with the other viands, which was, no doubt, found very acceptable. When it was necessary to depart, Clunes provided a boat for the fugitives, and Lochiel, who ventured to accompany them a part of the way. This boat was the only one in the district, as all the rest had been burnt to prevent the rebels from using them. Lochiel and the prince hesitated to cross the Lochy in the fragile, crazy craft, but Clunes at once volunteered to cross first with a batch of his friends, and, having done so safely, the prince and his party followed his example. In momentary terror that their route would be discovered, they made all haste to reach Glenbiasdale.

They arrived late in the evening of Saturday, the 19th of April, at the head of Loch Morar, where they resolved to remain, as darkness had come on, and the night promised to be wild and wet. They could find no human dwelling wherein to take shelter, until at last one of the party stumbled upon a lonely little hovel in the corner of a wood, which had been used at the sheep-shearing. There was no seat, table, nor stool in it, but Burke contrived to kindle a fire with turfs which lay in a corner, and having made seats of stones, the party passed the night as well as they could. As there was no boat at Loch Morar to ferry them across, they had no alternative but to walk round it on foot, and to cross steep and rugged ranges of mountains to accomplish their journey, which they did with great difficulty, arriving at Arasaig in the evening.

The prince now became really sensible that he was in a position of great jeopardy, and that some means must be resorted to immediately for his safety. Time was rapidly passing away, and the encroachments of the vigilant enemy were becoming hourly more imminent. It was therefore absolutely necessary that a prompt determination should be come to as to the royal fugitive's future movements. There the prince stood with his friends in deep meditation, in close vicinity to the place where he had originally landed on his arrival on the mainland. Lockhart, younger of Carnwath; young Clanranald; Æneas Macdonell, a banker in Paris; and several other devoted adherents were present, and a council was held as to what ought to be done. It was the prince's own desire to go to the Outer Hebrides, but his friends sternly objected, giving as a reason that government cruisers had been already ordered to scour all the lochs, bays, and channels of those regions, and that, in consequence, the chance of his being seized was much greater than if he remained on the mainland.

The meeting pondered in deep suspense, and their almost unanimous decision nearly prevailed on the prince to remain where he was, under the protection of his kind and faithful adherents. O'Sullivan alone objected, and eloquently insisted on the propriety of resorting to the Isles. He strenuously maintained that such was the only course that afforded any chance whatever of obtaining a vessel to convey His Royal Highness to France. The discussion became excited and warm; when one of those present addressed O'Sullivan, and openly accused him of previous gross mismanagement in the prince's cause. This was held to be confirmed by a letter from Lord George Murray to Charles, dated at Ruthven on 17th April, 1746, of which the following is an extract:—

I must also acquaint Your Royal Highness that we are all fully convinced that Mr. O'Sullivan, whom Your Royal Highness trusted with the most essential things with regard to your operations, was exceedingly unfit for it, and committed gross blunders on every occasion of moment. He whose business it was, did not so much as visit the ground where we were to be drawn up in line of battle, and it was a fatal error to allow the enemy these walls upon their left, which made it impossible for us to break them; and they, with their front fire, and flanking us when we went upon the attack, destroyed us, without any possibility of our breaking them, and our Athole men have lost a full half of their officers and men. I wish Mr. O'Sullivan had never got any other charge in the army than the care of the baggage, which, I am told, he had been brought up to, and understood. I never saw him in time of action neither at Gladsmuir, Falkirk, nor in the last, and his orders were vastly confused.

In this letter Lord George Murray made no secret of the estimate which he had formed of the prince's advisers, and particularly of O'Sullivan. His lordship was greatly chagrined at the unhappy course which events had taken, but attributed the whole misfortune to the mismanagement of parties who had usurped an authority which they were unable to exercise with prudence. Lord Murray, disgusted with the whole proceedings, determined to incur no more responsibility in a matter of such vast importance. He accordingly sent the prince a resignation of his command, remarking that he hoped the great cause might still be attended with better success. He had no idea that the war would then be abandoned, seeing that nearly two thousand Highlanders and others had assembled at Ruthven, expressing a determination to stand steadfast to the cause of their country and prince, and cordially to unite with chieftains and clansmen who might come forward to commence the campaign again.

The prince, as if diffident or ashamed to give prompt orders to his Ruthven friends to disperse at once, commenced to palliate matters, by stating that he was too powerless and weak to ensure success in the meantime, but that if he got safely to France, he would, no doubt, receive effectual aid in men and money to enable him to maintain the struggle, until happily he might obtain the victory. His communication, though couched in pleasing and plausible terms, yet breathed an air of despondency; and his friends at once construed it, in the words of Chambers:

As the death-note of the war. Accordingly, taking a melancholy leave of each other, they dispersed—the gentlemen to seek concealment in, or escape from, the country, and the common people to return to their homes.

The prince received Lord George Murray's letter by a messenger when in the midst of his deliberations, with his friends at Borrodale, as to his future movements. It is very probable that he had shown it to those devoted adherents around him, if not to O'Sullivan himself, whose reputation as an officer was so sharply commented on by Lord Murray. Be this as it may, the prince yielded to O'Sullivan's suggestion, and expressed a determination to seek refuge in the Western Isles.

When His Royal Highness, before the Battle of Culloden, entered the town of Inverness he met in private with several friends warmly attached to his person, and sincerely zealous in his cause. He happened to state that he expected some French vessels to arrive on the West Coast with money and requisite munitions of war, but was at a loss how to procure a trustworthy person to fall in with these foreign ships and get some of these requisites privately conveyed to him. His Royal Highness was informed by Banker Macdonell that he had just seen a faithful, worthy Skyeman in town whom he considered a most suitable person for the purpose required, if he would engage to do it.

The prince expressed a desire to see him; whereupon, in a short time, Macdonell brought Donald Macleod of Galtrigal into the presence of His Royal Highness, who shook hands with the humble Hebridean, and spent nearly an hour in conversation with him in a close in Church Street, near the Gaelic Church, wherein shortly afterwards, a number of poor rebels were imprisoned by the cruel Cumberland, and thence taken to the adjoining churchyard, where they were made to kneel down in rows, and were shot to death by a party of Cumberland's soldiers. With the view of making a sure aim, the unfortunate Highlanders were fired at by the soldiers placing their muskets on erect stones, which are still left standing as monuments of this most heart-rending cruelty.

Donald Macleod, an intelligent, enterprising man, was at the time in Inverness, loading a vessel with meal for Skye, and other places on the West Coast. Owing to Donald's knowledge of the Western Isles, he so far yielded to the prince's wishes, as to promise that he would accompany Banker Æneas Macdonell to Barra, to bring to His Royal Highness whatever money or despatches might have been left for him in that island. (An account of Donald Macleod's character, and his history, is in the *Celtic Magazine*, No. 19, Vol. II.).

These proposals of the prince with Galtrigal were not, however, put into execution, as, soon afterwards, the bloody engagement at Culloden took place, and nothing more was heard of Donald Macleod until the meeting of the prince with his adherents at Borrodale, when His Royal Highness, as already stated, expressed his determination to resort to the Western Isles. In the midst of their deliberations Macdonell informed the prince that Donald Macleod, whom he had seen at Inverness, had fortunately arrived with his vessel at Kinlochmoidart, and that of all men he knew, he would be the most suitable for conducting the intended cruise to the Hebrides. Chambers states that:

> A message was sent to Kinlochmoidart, where Donald now was, pressingly desiring him to come to meet the prince at Borrodale. Donald immediately set out, and, in passing through the forest of Glenbiasdale, he encountered a stranger walking by himself, who, making up to him, asked if he was Donald Macleod of Galtrigal? Donald, instantly recognising him notwithstanding his mean attire, said, 'I am the same man, please Your Highness; at your service'. 'Then,' said the prince, 'you see, Donald, I am in distress; I therefore throw myself into your bosom, and let you do with me what you like. I hear you are an honest man, and fit to be trusted'

When the old man, a year after, related these particulars to the individual who has reported them, the tears were streaming down his cheeks like rain.

The prince then proposed that Donald should go with letters from him to Sir Alexander Macdonald at Monkstadt, and to Macleod of Dunvegan, soliciting their protection. Donald stared His Royal Highness in the face, and said, "Is Your Royal Highness really in earnest in making such a mad request? The chiefs mentioned, you must be aware, are your enemies, and are at this moment employed in searching for you in the Isles and elsewhere."

"Well, well, Donald," said the prince, "all things seem to be adverse to me, but my good friend, you must at all events pilot me, and that immediately, to the Long Island."

Donald at once replied that he was ready to be of any service in his power, and risk his very life in his behalf—but that he peremptorily declined to be the bearer of any message to "the two apostate chiefs of Skye".

In order to put the prince's plan into execution with all possible speed, the most expert seamen and the most substantial boat in the place were procured and equipped at Borrodale, in the bay of Loch-nan-uagh, near the spot the prince first landed at on his arrival in Scotland. The office of captain, or headman, was delegated by common consent to Donald of Galtrigal, who was to steer and pilot the frail barque on the perilous voyage.

On the evening of the 26th of April the prince, O'Neil, O'Sullivan, and others, seated themselves in the boat, but Donald Macleod, leaning on the gunwale before entering the boat, and casting his eyes on the murky clouds all round, addressed the prince, saying, that the evening looked gloomy; that he did not like the bright, but black-edged openings in the clouds; that he was certain that a storm would arise; and that it was more prudent by far to remain for the night where they were. Charles absolutely refused, and said, "No, no, Donald, we will push on, and dread no evil while you sit at the helm".

On hearing this, Donald, very much against his will, ordered the sails to be set, while he himself took his place at the helm. In a few minutes the boat glided swiftly along, under a breeze portentously fresh. In less than an hour after, a terrible storm arose, with thunder and lightning; and the crew of seven men, besides the pilot, had more than enough to do to keep the boat from swamping.

The crested waves rose around like dark rolling mountains, and, breaking into the frail vessel in gushing streams, gave the crew very hard work to bale them out. Rain fell in torrents, and the brooding darkness like a gloomy curtain of death, was momentarily illuminated by the bright flashes of lightning that darted from cloud to cloud around! Sorely did the prince repent of his rashness and obstinacy in not yielding to the prudent advice of his sage and experienced pilot, but it was too late; and all that now remained was to try to make the best of it.

They had no compass, no chart, and scarcely any hope of safety. They could avoid neither rock, nor island, nor shore, nor quicksand; but were compelled to dash on before a sweeping Easterly hurricane, and trust to Providence. The prince, greatly impressed with the danger, frequently addressed the pilot, and said "Oh! Donald, Donald, I fear that all is over with us; this is worse than Culloden by far". Donald replied, that while they were afloat there was hope, and that He who had the winds and the waves under His command, was able to preserve them if they placed confidence in Him. Such was the case, for at daybreak, much to their surprise and their great joy, they observed the hills of the Long Island straight ahead, and in less than an hour after, they landed in a creek at Rossinish, on the east side of Benbecula, where they, with great difficulty, secured their boat, and their lives. The natives observing their approach, immediately assembled, and heartily assisted the weary mariners by conducting them to a place of safety.

It is scarcely necessary to say that the departure of the prince from Loch-nan-uagh, when it became known to the Duke of Cumberland, caused great consternation among the Royalists. They became mightily alarmed, not knowing what the consequences might be should the prince find access to the Highland chiefs and his adherents; for Cumberland was well aware, that, although he was so far successful at Culloden, that there existed a desire among the prince's friends to rally and to commence the campaign anew. The duke therefore gave immediate orders to provide cruisers, sloops of war, and all available sailing craft, to scour the Western seas, to convey troops to the Isles, and search every creek and corner, to find the royal fugitive dead or alive.

On the mainland the most cruel and heart-rending atrocities were committed on the helpless rebels! Men, women, and children, were murdered in cold blood, and mercy was extended to none. High and low became the victims of those ministers of vengeance and bloodshed! Like fiends of darkness they traversed the country from end to end, while silence, ruin, and death followed in their train. Mothers and matrons, sons and sires, infants and aged, were promiscuously massacred, or banished from the smoking ashes of their burning dwellings. Thus cruelly pursued, they had no alternative but to die of cold and hunger on the moors, or to perish in mountain recesses and in the caves of the rocks. The rebel chiefs were doomed by the Royalists, as far as possible, to the same fate. The castles and strongholds of Cluny, Keppoch, Glengyle, Glengarry, Lochiel, and many besides, were plundered and burnt to the ground. The devastations committed by the English Army were a stain on humanity, and were so notoriously cruel that the mere record of them will prove revolting in every age, and painful to every generous mind.

Meanwhile Prince Charles had commenced his wanderings in the Western Isles, where he ran many hair-breadth escapes for his life. It is unnecessary here to give a narrative of his various movements during his hazardous pilgrimage in the Long Island. (Further information on these points *vide* Chambers's *History of the Rebellion,* Brown's *History of the Highland Clans,* Cameron's *History and Traditions of the Isle of Skye, Jacobite Memoirs, Culloden Papers,* &c.)

He had been but a short time on shore, when many steadfast friends came to know that His Royal Highness was on the island in concealment. His whereabouts were always known to someone or other of his faithful adherents. His well-wishers in the place were numerous, and of considerable influence. Among them were Clanranald and his brother Boisdale, Banker Macdonell, Mr. O'Sullivan, Mr. O'Neal, the Macdonalds of Baileshear, and his own *"fidus Achates,"* Donald Macleod of Galtrigal. Clanranald and his excellent lady had selected twelve trusty men, whom they had sworn to fidelity, to act as messengers and guides to His Royal Highness on every emergency when their services were required.

Day after day the danger increased and rendered the situation of the royal fugitive more and more critical. Of all this he was fully aware, yet he appeared cheerful and apparently unconcerned in the presence of his friends. By sea and land every imaginable precaution was taken, by commands from headquarters, to prevent the possibility of his escape. Every ferry was guarded, and every pass and highway had sentinels planted in them. About two thousand regular troops and militiamen were posted in suitable localities. The whole range of country was so thoroughly watched, that the least movement on the part of the natives could hardly escape immediate observation. The various lochs and bays by which the Long Island is indented, as well as the open Atlantic surrounding it, were so thickly studded with cutters and cruisers, frigates and sloops of war, that no craft, however small, could approach or leave the island unobserved.

At last the danger became so imminent that the prince's friends held a consultation at Ormiclade, the residence of Clanranald, as to the adoption of some immediate steps for his preservation, if such could at all be effected. After weighing the matter from every point of view, it was ultimately agreed that an attempt should be made to effect his rescue through the instrumentality of a young lady in the neighbourhood, Miss Flora Macdonald of Milton.

Let us now leave His Royal Highness in his cave in the rocky recesses of Corrodale, (see note following), while we will attempt to delineate the early history and future movements of this interesting young lady.

✶✶✶✶✶✶

The recess or cave where the prince was concealed was about ten miles from Ormiclade, at a place called Corrodale, on the east side of Béinn Mhor, near the point of Uisinish, and situated between Loch Boisdale and Loch Skipport. The spot is rugged, wild, and sequestered, and almost inaccessible to strangers.

✶✶✶✶✶✶

CHAPTER 3

Flora's Family, Youth, and Education

Flora Macdonald was the daughter of Ranald Macdonald, younger of Milton, in South Uist. She was born in 1722, being thus two years younger than the prince. She was patronimically designated "Fionnghal nighean Raonuill 'ic Aonghais Oig, an Airidh Mhuilinn"; that is, "Flora the daughter of Ranald the son of Angus, younger of Milton". Ranald was a cadet of the family of Clanranald, and not very distantly related. Flora's mother was Marion, daughter of the Rev. Angus Macdonald, for some years Parish minister of the Island of Gigha, but afterwards translated to South Uist. He was designated "Aonghas Mac Uistein Ghriminish," that is, "Angus son of Hugh of Griminish," in the Island of North Uist.

This clergyman was noted in the country as a man of extraordinary muscular strength. He had no equal in the place for lifting ponderous weights, or for any of those athletic exercises requiring great bodily power. He was a mild, generous, and much respected gentleman. The natives of the Hebrides were always noted for their attention and kindness to strangers, but the Rev. Angus Macdonald was proverbial for his genuine Highland hospitality. He was known in the island as "A Ministear làidir," or "The Strong Minister," and the name was by no means misapplied. His wife was a talented and accomplished lady, a daughter of Macdonald of Largie, in Kintyre. Flora was the only daughter of the family, but she had two brothers.

The elder, Ranald, was a very promising youth, who appeared to inherit no small portion of his reverend grandfather's activity and strength. He on one occasion paid a visit to his relatives at Largie, where the gallant youth lost his life by the bursting of a blood vessel. It is said that he strained himself by rowing a boat against an adverse wind, and this caused his death, to the deep regret of a numerous circle of relatives and friends.

Flora's younger brother, Angus, succeeded his father at Milton, while her mother, in 1728, married, as her second husband, Hugh Macdonald of Armadale in Skye, a Captain of Militia in the Long Island during the prince's wanderings there. (*Vide* account of Hugh Macdonald of Armadale in No. xx.,Vol. II., *Celtic Magazine*. Armadale is situated in the Parish of Sleat in the south end of Skye, and is the residence of the "Macdonalds of the Isles").

Had it not been for the friendly disposition of Hugh Macdonald towards the prince, in all probability His Royal Highness could never have effected his escape from the Long Island. Through Hugh's instrumentality, which will be referred to hereafter, the prince was rescued, and it is thought that his friends, with all their ingenuity, would have utterly failed to devise any other plan or scheme whereby his life could have been saved.

When Flora's mother, after her marriage, was about to remove to her new residence in Skye, she naturally desired to take her little and only daughter along with her, but her son, Milton, then a full grown youth, and an active manager of the place, felt extremely reluctant to part with his sister. She was only two years of age when she lost her father, and six years at the date of her mother's second marriage. The mother and son could not at all agree as to the little girl. After much talking and reasoning with each other regarding her removal to Skye with her mother, they utterly failed to agree. It was then determined to leave the issue to the decision of young Flora herself; and being asked whether she preferred to accompany her mother to Skye, or remain with her brother at Milton? she smartly replied:

> I will stay at Milton because I love it. I do not know Skye, and
> do not care for it I will therefore remain with Angus until my
> dear mamma comes back for me.

Flora was a most interesting child, wise beyond her years, and more sage in her remarks than the generality of children. No doubt this arose from the circumstances of there being no children in the family at Milton whom she associated with, and of her growing up accustomed only to the conversation, ideas, and society of persons of maturer years. But in addition to all this, she was naturally a precocious little girl, who showed an early taste for the beautiful, great, and grand in nature. She had been known to stand for hours admiring the battling of the elements, when the bold Atlantic rose in mountains of foam.

It was a magnificent sight to behold the storm in its fury dashing on the western shores of the island, and showering its briny spray over the length and the breadth of the land. The whole scenery of the place, with the grandeur of the surrounding isles, could never fail to arouse feelings of admiration in the minds of young or old, who possessed the sensibility of discerning the variegated beauties of nature.

It is therefore a matter of certainty that any worshipper at the shrine of Nature, will find ample materials to indulge his fancy in the solitude of this interesting Isle. On the west is the frowning Atlantic, with its chilling breeze and stern aspect, even in the heat and calm of summer; but alas! in winter the scene is mightily changed. At that season, the sleeping deep arises in fury, and dashes forward in monster waves, as if to engulf in ruin the intervening rocks and plains of the adjacent land.

At times the lonely St. Kilda is visible in the dim horizon like a huge beacon in the midst of the crested waves, or like an unearthly spectre rearing its hideous head amid the green billows, to foster the superstitions of a race of honest, simple natives, naturally impressible with such scenes. Then turning towards the east, the Minch, in its wide expanse, appears dotted with ships and craft of all calibre and size. Further on in the same direction, at a distance of thirty to forty miles, Skye rears its misty cliffs; and high above the surrounding mountains, the rugged, serrated outlines of the Cuchullin hills are seen darting into the clouds. On either side and all around the scenery is variegated, beautiful, and in some parts really magnificent.

In a beautiful poem, by "Fear Gheasto," entitled *Farewell to Skye*, the chief mountain scenery of that far-famed Isle is exceedingly well described; and as it is the scenery which our heroine admired from her earlier years, a *stanza* or two may be given:—

Farewell, lovely Skye, sweet Isle of my childhood,
Thy blue mountains I'll clamber no more;
Thy heath-skirted corries, green valleys and wildwood,
I now leave behind for a far distant shore.
Adieu, ye stern cliffs, clad in old hoary grandeur,
Adieu, ye still dingles, fond haunts of the roe,
Where oft with my gun, and my hounds I did wander,
And echo loud sounded to my "tally-ho".

How painful to part from the misty-robed Coollin,
The Alps of Great Britain, with antlered peaks high;

Bold Glamaig, Coruisk, and sublime Scuirnagillin,
Make mainland grand mountains, look dull, tame and shy.
Majestic Quiraing, fairy palace of Nature,
Stormy Idrigill, Hailleaval, and cloud piercing Stoer,
And the shining Spar-cave like some beacon to heaven,
All, I deeply lament, and may never see more!

Once more, dearest Isle, let me gaze on thy mountains,
Once more, let the village church gleam on my view;
And my ear drink the music of murmuring fountains,
While I bid to my old, and my young friend, adieu.
Farewell, lovely Skye, lake, mountain, and corrie;
Brown Isle of the valiant, the brave, and the free;
Ever green to thy sad, resting place of my Flora,
My sighs are for Skye, my tears are for thee.

Such then is the locality where the famous Flora first came into the world, and such the scenes on which she daily cast her eyes. She was, when a mere girl, not only a favourite with all her own more intimate associates, but with every respectable family in the place. Being an only daughter, and left fatherless at so early an age, created no doubt a general feeling of sympathy in her favour. All this, together with her agreeable behaviour, although a mere child, rendered her proverbial in the place, and caused her name to be generally brought forward, as an example, by parents in correcting their children, asking them, "C'uin a bhios sibh cosmhuil ri Fionnghal Nighean Roanuill, an Airidh-Mhuilinn?" "When will you resemble Flora of Milton!" She was naturally smart, clever, and active, but cautious in her movements, and was invariably the principal or leader in every game, or juvenile frolic in which she engaged.

She was, in every respect, a most interesting girl, and she became a particular favourite with all the respectable families in the Island, especially with Clanranald and his lady, his brother Boisdale and family, and her own relatives at Baileshear. Lady Clanranald acted towards her more like a mother than a distant relative She was seldom left at home with her brother at Milton, but paid long visits to her friends in the district, and these visits were welcomed by all.

When she was about thirteen years of age, Lady Clanranald insisted on her remaining continuously at Ormiclade, that she might get the benefit of instruction from a governess who had been provided by Clanranald for his own children. Such was the kindness of the family at Ormiclade, that she could not express her gratitude. For about three years her home was in the hospitable mansion of Clanranald, with the exception of occasional short trips to Skye, to visit her mother at Armadale. She by far excelled in her lessons the daughters of the family, and although Clanranald and his lady had too much sense not to appreciate her expertness and aptitude for the acquisition of useful instruction, yet their daughters in some degree became jealous of poor Flora, and hinted that the governess was more attentive to her than to them. There was every appearance that, in their hearts, the youngsters at Ormiclade cherished a certain degree of envy towards the unoffending *protégé*.

Flora was by far too clear-sighted not to see all this, and too prudent not to be able to effect a remedy. She endured everything patiently for about half-a-year, as in reality the youngsters only had taken private offence at her success, while the parents very probably had never thought or heard anything about it. She had given intimation in her own pleasing and grateful way to Lady Clanranald, that by such a time, she would require to visit her mother, and spend some time with her, as she, again and again, heard herself charged with being an unnatural daughter, and very undutiful for having deserted her only parent, and lost all sense of her filial duties. "Eh! me, Flora dear," said Lady Clanranald, "what will become of 'Ceolag,' if you go off and leave us, and what will become of us all? If you do go, you must return soon, and bear that in mind."

This "Ceolag" to which allusion is made, was the name given in the family to a spinet, or small piano at Ormiclade, on which Flora became an astonishing performer. She acquired a knowledge of the notes from the governess, but her own correct ear for music, was the real source of her success. She could play not only the reels and the dance music of the day with no ordinary efficiency, but also the ancient *piobaireachds*, in which she gave due prominence to all the *pogiaturas* and grace-notes of the quick variations. In the same manner, even at her youthful age, she could sing Gaelic songs exceedingly well, and repeat lengthy strains of ancient poetry in that language. All these she committed to memory from the rehearsals of the bards and seanachies who then existed in the Isles.

In 1739, Lady Clanranald had a communication from Lady Margaret Macdonald (wife of Sir Alexander Macdonald of the Isles, residing at Monkstadt, in Skye), expressing a wish to have a visit from Flora, whom her ladyship had not seen for two years. She desired this visit to take place for a praiseworthy purpose, which she intimated to Lady Clanranald, and which was to the effect, that she and her husband, Sir Alexander, were desirous that Flora should be well educated, and that they had certain plans in view for that purpose, which they hoped soon to be able to execute.

Flora appeared much gratified at this act of attention by Sir Alexander's lady, although as yet she was entirely ignorant of the special purposes which her ladyship had in view regarding her. She had been frequently at Monkstadt before, where she met with as much kindness from her noble chief and his lady as if she had been their own child. She therefore formed the idea that her presence was wanted in Skye, with the view, perhaps, to place her under the tuition of some notable teacher who may have come to the castle.

It may be remarked that in Skye at that period all kinds of useful education flourished in respectable families beyond most other quarters of the Highlands. The cause was this:—Public schools were few in number, but the gentlemen farmers procured for themselves a remedy for this inconvenience. They resorted to a very successful expedient for counteracting the existing deficiency in the means of education. It so happened that a century or a century and a-half ago, farmers of the middle class, or such as rented lands to an extent that enabled them to be ranked as gentlemen, were very numerous in Skye, though now, alas! the very reverse is the case. These snug, comfortable, moderately-rented tenements have been, since then, conjoined into extensive deer forests or into large sheep walks. The consequence is, that now one sheep-farmer occupies a tract of pasture, which in past ages afforded means of support to twenty, thirty, or fifty respectable and well-to-do middleclass tenants.

These tenants, prudent, sagacious men, to educate their families, clubbed together and engaged a common tutor, perhaps a well recommended student of Divinity, or some learned young gentleman from the south of Scotland, and sometimes even from England. By this arrangement every group of contiguously situated families had their centrical schoolroom, nicely fitted up, their qualified teacher, and their children thus efficiently educated in the common, and often in the higher branches of knowledge. Hence the vast number, within the last century and a-half, from that Island, who had distinguished themselves so much in the civil and military services of their king and country. No other territory of the extent of Skye, in the whole kingdom or elsewhere, can boast of one-half the number of distinguished

35

men, in all the departments of the public service, as Skye can do.

★★★★★★

A good many years ago, a correct and elaborate computation was made on competent authority, that during the wars with America and France, from the middle of the past to the beginning of the present century, the Isle of Skye furnished the following remarkable number of men for the service of their sovereign, *viz.*:—10,000 foot soldiers, 500 pipers, 600 commissioned officers, under the rank of Colonel, 48 Lieutenant-Colonels, 21 Lieutenant-Generals and Major-Generals, 4 Governors of British Colonies, 1 Governor-General, 1 Adjutant-General, 1 Chief Baron of England, and 1 Judge of the Supreme Court of Scotland. Besides this a great number filled offices in the University, in the Church, and in legal departments.

★★★★★★

In some of these excellent schools Flora received the ground-work of her education. Owing to this, and to the excellent training of which she had the benefit under the hospitable roof of Lady Clanranald, her mind was, at a comparatively early age, well stored with rudimental knowledge, as well as deeply imbued with a veneration for the Highland system of clanship, and with loyalty to the exiled house of Stuart.

According to the request of Lady Margaret, preparations were made for Flora's departure to Skye, by the first favourable opportunity that offered itself of a safe passage across the Minch, (The name of the channel which intervenes between the Long Island and Skye, which is from 20 to 30 miles in breadth, and is frequently very rough and stormy). It happened at this time that a sort of pirate ship frequented the creeks and bays of the Long Island, by means of which many persons of both sexes were cajoled on board, made prisoners, and deprived of their liberty.

At these wicked proceedings the natives of the Lews, Harris, Uist, Benbecula, and Skye became exceedingly alarmed, and it created much anxiety and confusion among all ranks and classes of the natives. The authorities in these quarters resorted to every measure within their power to counteract this base and unlooked-for cruelty. Unfortunately, however, the leader of the kidnapping party managed to set sail for the Southern States of America with a shipload of his own country-people of all ages, with the intention of selling them into slavery. While the united efforts of all the authorities, lay and clerical, seemed to be of no avail to check it, an overruling Providence immediately intervened to put a speedy termination to the cruel and unchristian procedure. Soon after the pirate ship had sailed from the shores of the Long Island with its cargo of innocent natives, a terrific gale sprung up, which dashed the unhallowed ship into a rocky creek on the coast of Ireland, where it was totally wrecked, and splintered into fragments.

All the prisoners escaped as if by a miracle, without the loss of a single life; and through the kindness of Irish philanthropists they were humanely cared for, and eventually conveyed to their homes. It was soon afterwards discovered that the chief leader in this diabolical plot was a young man, Norman Macleod, son of Donald Macleod, tacksman of the Island of Berneray. The stern-hearted youth escaped the punishment which his dastardly deeds so richly merited, by crossing *incognito* to Ireland, where he concealed himself for about two years. He subsequently joined himself to the government forces, and was soon raised to the rank of captain. In the course of a few years he became a changed and much-respected man, succeeded his father at Berneray, and died there at the ripe age of nearly a hundred years.

Along with all others, Lady Margaret Macdonald deeply shared in the general alarm created by his wicked conduct. Her ladyship did so the more, no doubt, from a private report that got into circulation, that her husband, Sir Alexander, had some secret hand in the cruel undertaking, in order to get the people away, and to banish them from his extensive estates. Knowing well her husband's innocence in this painful matter, her ladyship became quite indignant, and greatly disturbed in her peace of mind. In his absence, she addressed a long letter, dated 1st January, 1740, to Lord Justice-Clerk Milton, in which she gave a long and minute detail of the whole affair. She assured his Lordship that Sir Alexander:

> Was both angry and deeply concerned to hear that some of his own people were taken away in this manner, but could not at the time learn who were the actors in this wicked scrape until the ship was gone.

Her ladyship's letter was long and interesting, and may be seen in the *Culloden Papers*.

When the existence of this piratical vessel was noised abroad, sloops and craft of every description were sent by the authorities in Skye to the Long Island, but too late to seize the expected prize. Being in the dead of winter, the weather was boisterous and wild, and

WOMEN AT THE QUERN AND PULING CLOTH, WITH A VIEW OF TALISKER

the different vessels had to lie at anchor in the lochs and bays of the Island. It was, however, arranged that in one of them Flora was to be accommodated with a passage to Skye, to the hospitable residence of Lady Margaret at Monkstadt One evening she set sail in one of the largest of the craft, and the night being stormy the vessel was driven into Loch Snizort, and anchored about sunrise at the "Crannag," near the mansion-house of Kingsburgh.

Flora was glad to get ashore, but finding that the Kingsburgh family were absent at Flodigarry, she walked a few miles to the house of Penduin, the residence of Captain Norman Macleod, the very house in which, after an eventful life, she died about fifty years afterwards. Next day she made the best of her way to the residence of Sir Alexander at Monkstadt, about fourteen miles distant She was warmly received by Lady Margaret, with whom she remained about eight months, with the exception of a short stay of a few weeks with her mother at Armadale.

Lady Margaret felt a deep interest in Flora's welfare, and she was much pleased with her prudence, general conduct, and amiable disposition. In due course she fully revealed her plans to her, and explained that she and Sir Alexander had arranged to pass the winter in Edinburgh, and that she had resolved that Flora should accompany them and finish her education in the metropolis. Flora gratefully acknowledged her ladyship's kindness, and modestly signified her willingness to comply. She then visited her mother, and intimated to her the kind intentions of Lady Margaret, and, obtaining her consent, which the old lady readily granted, she bade her mother farewell, returned to Monkstadt; and, matters being settled for the removal to Edinburgh, she seized the first opportunity of crossing the channel to Ormiclade, and to her brother at Milton.

It was proposed by Lady Margaret that Flora should visit the metropolis during the autumn of that season, but circumstances occurred to prevent that arrangement. Lady Clanranald was an invalid at the time, as was also Flora's brother Angus, at Milton, in both cases from neglected colds. Such being the case, Flora's kind, generous heart would not permit her to leave these friends in a state of inconvalescence; and there was a remarkable providence in her resolve, for the sloop by which she proposed to sail to Glasgow was wrecked on the Mull of Cantyre, on her passage to Edinburgh, and not a single life was saved.

Fortunately, in course of time her invalid friends recovered of their ailments, and Flora resided at Ormiclade and Milton during the winter and spring. Early in the following summer (1740) she embraced another opportunity of visiting her friends in Skye. Throughout that Island she was welcomed by every family of respectability, but particularly so by those at Scorribreck, Kingsburgh, Cuiderach, and Monkstadt. Arrangements were now made for her departure to Edinburgh during the ensuing months of September or October, according to the state of the weather, as by that time Lady Margaret and Sir Alexander expected to reach the metropolis themselves.

About the beginning of August, Flora bade farewell to her friends in Skye, and revisited her native Isle, which, of all localities, was the most dear to her Highland heart. Towards the end of September, she took her passage from Uist to Glasgow in a small schooner belonging to the place, laden with cured cod and ling for the southern markets. The captain's name was Roderick Macdonald, usually called "Ruairidh Muideartach," being a native of Moidart, on the mainland. Rory was a very jolly, middle-aged tar, who materially diminished the tediousness of the passage by his singing of Gaelic songs, in which he could not easily be excelled. In this respect he met with a very congenial spirit in his only cabin passenger, Flora being one who greatly admired the Celtic muse of her skipper.

At length, after an ordinary passage, the schooner arrived safely at what is now called the Broomielaw of Glasgow. Two days after, Flora found her way by some public conveyance to Edinburgh. On her arrival at that city, where she was an entire stranger, she resorted with as little delay as possible to a boarding-school provided for her through the kind services of Lady Margaret This Ladies' Seminary, which was attended by about half-a-dozen of other young ladies, was taught by a Miss Henderson, in the Old Stamp-Office Close, High Street, near the town residence of the Earl of Eglinton. The Countess of Eglinton and her daughters usually resided in Edinburgh during the winter months; and Flora had been only a few days in her new seminary when some of these noble ladies did her the honour of visiting her at Miss Henderson's. She was agreeably surprised, but soon came to understand that they had done so by the instructions of Lady Margaret, who had not then arrived in town herself.

The Eglinton ladies were as much noted for their affability and kindness as they were celebrated for their personal beauty and charms. All the daughters were exceedingly handsome, and no doubt they had inherited these qualities from their mother, the Countess Susan Kennedy, who is said to have been one of the handsomest women of her day. It is recorded in the *Traditions of Edinburgh*, that:

> Countess Susan's daughters were all equally remarkable with herself for a good mien; and the 'Eglintoune air' was a common phrase at the time. It was a goodly sight a century ago to see the long procession of sedans, containing Lady Eglintoune and her daughters devolve from the Close, and proceed to the Assembly Rooms in the West Bow when there was usually a considerable crowd of plebeian admirers congregated to behold their lofty and graceful figures step from the chairs on the pavement. It could not fail to be a remarkable sight—eight beautiful women, conspicuous for their stature and carriage, all dressed in the splendid, though formal fashion of that period, and inspired at once with dignity of birth and consciousness of beauty.

During Flora's stay in Edinburgh, which lasted over three years continuously, she had the good fortune to be introduced to many families of high rank and distinction, such as Bishop Forbes of Leith, the Mackenzies of Delvin, and many others. The friendship that subsisted between the Delvin family and herself lasted during her lifetime. It may be stated to Flora's credit and great good sense, that notwithstanding the elevated rank of many of those into whose society and residence she had often been invited, and from whom she received much hospitality and attention, that she invariably conducted herself with such a degree of unassuming modesty as added materially to her appreciation in the eyes of others.

In prosperity and adversity, she ever retained the same equable temperament of mind—the same gentle, submissive deportment, and the same calm spirit of resignation and contentment. Whatever might have fallen to her lot, and many distressing things did, yet her frame of mind remained constantly unruffled and unchanged. While possessed of a keen, lively, sensitive nature, yet she was largely gifted with the power of exercising a complete control over her feelings, and of appearing on all occasions cheerful, pleasant, and entertaining.

Flora attended closely to her education in the seminary in which she was placed during the first two seasons of her stay in the metropolis. She considerably excelled her fellow pupils in the comparatively few branches of education in which instruction was communicated to females at that period. In the musical department, a sort of small harp was the instrument generally used for inculcating a knowledge of that interesting science. Flora, however, preferred to cultivate her taste in that respect by practising on a spinet or small pianoforte, at which she was out of sight the most proficient in the school.

From the correctness of her ear, she had acquired a facility in the use of this instrument—her own favourite "Ceolag" at Ormiclade—which enabled her to play, as already stated, a great variety of Highland airs and *piobaireachds* with a degree of grace and ease that delighted all around her. She was also gifted with a sweet, mellow voice, which rendered her capable of singing Gaelic songs exceedingly well, and much to the gratification and amusement of the company present. She was in consequence frequently asked the favour of singing those songs in the drawing-rooms of the noble and great, where no one present understood a single vocable of the *stanzas* she so sweetly sung.

Having passed nearly three seasons with the ladies in the Old Stamp-Office Close, under whose charge she was at first settled, she afterwards resided chiefly in the house of Lady Margaret and Sir Alexander, where her ladyship treated her as a member of her own family, and showed her as much maternal kindness as should she have been one of her daughters. Flora became so thoroughly domesticated and useful to her ladyship that she pressed upon her to prolong her stay in Edinburgh for more than a year after she had made up her mind to return to her mother, and her friends in the Long Island. Sir Alexander was not at that time in very robust health; and, by the advice of his medical attendants, he remained for about two years continuously in Edinburgh without returning to his residence in Skye. On two occasions Flora accompanied Lady Margaret to Eglinton Castle, where weeks were pleasantly spent under the noble roof of the ancient domicile in which her ladyship first saw the light of day.

The intelligence of the disastrous defeat of the British forces at Fontenoy soon after reached the Scottish Capital, and caused no ordinary alarm. In a few weeks rumours were prevalent that the victory gained by the French over the allied forces of Britain was hailed as a propitious event for the prospects of the young *chevalier* and his numerous partisans. As the days were passing, these rumours were gaining more and more feasibility in the eyes of the community at large. However clandestinely the Jacobites were devising their schemes, yet the reality of their purposes was hourly becoming more apparent to the loyal subjects of the reigning monarch of Great Britain. In short, the state of the country in connection with the well-known intrigues of the youthful aspirant to the British throne was the continual subject of conversation among the citizens of all classes.

★★★★★★

It was amusing to see and hear the citizens of Edinburgh, of all ranks and classes, standing in groups on the High Street, the Lawn Market, about old St. Giles, and other thoroughfares, keenly discussiug the events of the day, and fighting the battle of Fontenoy over again. Such dialogues as the following might then be heard:

Davie.—"Sad stirrin' news that, Jamie, in the *Courant* the day! Man, did ye see it?"

Jamie.—"No; what is't? I see lots o' folk speakin' awa' aboot some fearfu' thing that happint east awa', whar an unco feck were killt, but I kenna' whar."

Davie.—"Hut, man, didna' ye hear that a man cam' a the wai on horseback frae Lunnon, as fast as the creatur's heels coud carry him, to tell that maistly a our sodgers were killt by the French at some unco queer place o'er the sea, but I dinna min' the name o't?"

Jamie.—"Ye frichten me, Davie; is't a' gospel? Aiblins it may be a wheen o' lies. What does the *Courant* say about it?"

Davie.—"It's as true's death, Jamie; but didna' ye hear that a darin' chiel that they ca' the young Chevaleer is comin' o'er wi a' the French at his tail, to ding doon and sweep awa' our King and a' his big folks, and like his faither afore him, to fecht hard, that he may get to be our King himsel'?"

Jamie.—" Are ye tellin' what's richt, Davie? Will ye say 'Faith' that it's true? Surely that's the reason o' a' the steer and din that the folk are makin' in thir days on our streets. They're a' rinnin' aboot as gif the toun was on fire! Aye, and the provost himsel', and thae bodies o' Bailies o' his, scamperin' up and doon the streets as if they were clean crackit in their brains, for my certy, there's something awfu' in the wind. But what say ye aboot that loon the Chevaleer's faither, and whan was he in oor country fechtin' for the croon?"

Davie.—"O! Jamie, Jamie, my maun, I thocht ye had mair sense! Do ye nae mind that your ain coushin, Jenny Nelson's gudeman, was shot dead in yon bluidy battle near the toun o' Dumblane, aboot thirty year syne, and that battle was on account o' this mad loon's faither; but, Giridness be thankit, he made naething o't, and we hope that his son may male' still less?"

Jamie.—"But what richt hae thae callans wi' oor kingdom; we dinna trouble them?"

Davie.—"Weel, Jamie, there's nae doot they hae akin' o' richt throu' their bluid and kin in some wai that I canna explain, as it is sae unco raivellt and intercate, and I am nae gealogist; but nae doot they are Stuarts, ye ken, and they wanted to come in, but as they were Papists, we wad hae naething to dae wi' them."

Jamie.—"Waes me! Davie. It will be an awfu' thing, Guidness preserve us, gif we will hae war again in this oor ain countra, for as sure as death, Davie, I dinna like it ava! Eh! nae, nae."

★★★★★★

Sir Alexander Macdonald had much at stake, and should a revolution be attempted, his position was a critical one, which required no ordinary firmness of resolution, as well as a steadfast determination, to stand true to his king and country.

The worthy baronet, although far from being robust in health at the time, saw the necessity of making the best of his way to Skye, to be in readiness for whatever changes or events might come to pass. Flora was at the time on a visit to her kind friend Bishop Forbes at Leith, and a messenger was sent to her requesting her to return to Edinburgh without delay, as Sir Alexander and his lady were making ready for their journey to Skye, and that she of course was to accompany them. It was a matter of no ordinary concern to all by what means that long journey was to be accomplished, as the modes of transit were at that time very different from those of the present day. Sir Alexander in the meantime had fixed upon no particular plan as to how he and his party were to leave the Capital for the North, when he accidentally met with the Lord President Forbes of Culloden at a public dinner given by one of the Lords of Session.

In course of conversation about the alarming rumours that had reached from France in regard to the purposes of the young *chevalier*, the President stated that it was necessary that he should leave the city for Culloden, as matters of no ordinary importance might there require his immediate attention. Sir Alexander informed the President that he had similar intentions, and had judged it a prudent step, although his health was not what he would wish it to be, to return without delay to his clan and countrymen in Skye. The President told his friend, the baronet, that he had resolved to take passage to Inverness in the smack *Brothers*, commanded by an acquaintance of his own, a Captain Mackenzie, a cautious sailor, and a steady man. Sir Alexander made up his mind at once to accompany his friend by the same route, and matters were to be speedily arranged accordingly.

On the third day of June, the whole party went on board the *Brothers* in Leith harbour, and set sail on the evening of the same day. A suitable supply of the requisite creature comforts was put on board by Sir Alexander and the President, which proved a wise precaution, as the passage proved tedious. The weather was all that could be desired, but much too calm for a speedy voyage. There happened to be a numerous company on board, among the rest, Mr. John Fraser, Provost of Inverness, and two bailies of that borough, who had been in Edinburgh attending some legal proceedings connected with the town. The provost was a very facetious, jocular gentleman, whose mind was well stored with anecdotes, and whose art in telling them was easy and natural. He frequently kept the company in roars of laughter, and everything was most enjoyable and pleasant.

Lady Margaret was much taken with his interesting stories, and would now and then address him, saying, "Come now, Provost, tell us something else". Flora, naturally reserved, modest, and unassuming, appeared to enjoy the company exceedingly, and at intervals amused the company by singing some of her Gaelic songs. Of all on board, the captain of the smack seemed the most discontented. This arose from the tardy progress made by his comfortable vessel, in consequence of the continued calm. At length, after the lapse of fully eight days, the *Brothers* arrived safely at Inverness. The party went ashore with grateful thanks, but not until they had presented a few gifts to Captain Mackenzie for his unceasing attention to the comforts of his passengers.

Sir Alexander, before leaving Edinburgh, had written to his servants in Skye to send three horses properly saddled to Inverness, to convey Lady Margaret, Miss Flora, and himself to his residence in that island. At that time there were no public roads, but rough riding paths from Inverness to Skye, and, in consequence, the journey was very fatiguing and uncomfortable, particularly for ladies. Sir Alexander and his party passed a whole week very pleasantly in the Highland Capital, and were visited during their stay by most of the surrounding lairds, such as Grant of Glenmoriston, Baillie of Dochfour, Maclean of Dochgarroch, Robertson of Inshes, and several others. The worthy provost invited a large party of ladies and gentlemen to do him the honour of dining with him at his own residence.

Among other guests were the Lord President, Glenmoriston, Dochfour, and some of the aristocracy of the town. Ample justice was done to a substantial repast, and nothing less so to a hogshead of superior claret which the hospitable chief-magistrate had recently imported. A delightful evening was spent with anecdote and song, to the entertainment of which the modest Flora contributed no ordinary share. The whole company admired the beauty of her Gaelic melodies. She was naturally supposed by some of those present to be one of Sir Alexander's daughters, as Lady Margaret treated her with such motherly attention and kindness.

Glenmoriston received a promise from the island chief that, on his way to Skye, he would spend a day or two with him at his romantic residence, and make Glenmoriston his first stage from Inverness. The Grants of Glenmoriston were steadfast adherents to the reigning dynasty. Mr. Charles Fraser-Mackintosh, M.P., in *Antiquarian Notes*, states that:

> In the struggle that prevailed during the whole of the seventeenth and first half of the eighteenth centuries, the Grants of Glenmoriston invariably supported the Royal cause, while the chiefs as firmly ranged themselves on the other side. This much tended to support the independence of Glenmoriston, and many of Grant's people, particularly in Urquhart, were enthusiastic for the Stuarts.

Two days after, three saddled horses arrived in town to convey Sir Alexander, his lady, and Miss Flora to Skye. Each horse had his "Gilleceann-srein," or attendant, who walked on the right side of the horse to protect the rider.

★★★★★★

Every Highland Chief had a numerous staff of strong and robust "gillies," or attendants, to each of whom regular duties were prescribed. These were ten to twelve in number, such as the "Bladair," the fool, or jest-man; the "Piobair," the piper; the "Gilie-Piobair," the bearer of the piper's bag-pipe; the "Filidh," or bard, to sing his chieftain's praises; there was also the "Gille-Casfhlinch," being a strong man to carry his chief across morasses, streams, and rivers; the "Gille-Mor," the man to carry the chief's heavy broad-sword; the "Gille-Trusarnais," or the "Gille-Malaid," the baggage-man; the "Gille-ruith," the message-man; and the "Gille-ceann-srein," the man who guarded and led the horse when the chief was riding.

★★★★★★

The party on leaving Inverness by the rough mountainous path by Kinmylies, and through Caiplich, Abriachan, and Glen-Urquhart, arrived safely that evening at Invermoriston House, where they remained for two days enjoying the chief's hospitality with a select company of guests. The next route was by Cluany and Glenshiel. At the latter place, on account of a heavy rainfall, by which the mountain rivulets were swollen into impassable streams, they had to pass the night in a small inn, where they received all the comforts that the little Highland hostelry could afford. Starting early the following morning, they went through Kintail, crossed Kyleakin ferry into Skye, and arrived late in the evening at the hospitable house of Corriechatachain, where the Mackinnon of the day gladly welcomed his unexpected guests.

★★★★★★

Dr. Samuel Johnson, about twenty-eight years after, was greatly pleased with the kind reception that he met with on his visit to Corriechatachain, as may be seen in Dr. Carruthers' interesting notes appended to Boswell's tour to the Hebrides. Mackinnon of Corriechatachain was of an old sept of that clan, whose descendants lately claimed the chieftainship. Many well versed in the genealogical branches of the clan, were of opinion that the claim was well founded. The last male representative of this sept was the late Mr. A. K. Mackinnon of Corry, who was for many years factor to Lord Macdonald, and only died a few years ago, (as at 1882).

★★★★★★

Miss Flora was more than delighted to find her venerable mother at Corriechatachain, with the expectation of meeting there with Sir Alexander and his party. She had come from her own residence at Armadale, a distance of about twenty miles, to welcome her daughter back to Skye after so long an absence. In two days more, Sir Alexander and his party, with their retinue, arrived safely at the family residence at Monkstadt, whither Miss Flora's mother accompanied them.

CHAPTER 4

Flora and the Prince in the Long Island

It often occurs that qualities and virtues in the female character are utterly unknown to the world at large, merely because no event had ever taken place to afford an opportunity of displaying them. Such qualities and virtues elicit no remark, perhaps, when displayed by persons in a private sphere of life, whereas such amiable endowments often become of great importance when exhibited by such as may be called upon to perform some important public duty. Such was exactly the case with Miss Flora Macdonald. Had it not been that her prudence and energies were called forth by the important and critical part which she was instrumental in achieving, she might have lived and died unknown to the world.

It is true that she was a young lady naturally gifted with an amiable disposition, firm determination, wide sympathies, an affectionate nature, and a strong sense of personal duty; but other young Highland ladies might have been similarly endowed, of whom nothing was ever heard or known beyond the sphere of their acquaintance, or the more contracted circle of their immediate relatives and friends. It was not so, however, with the kind-hearted heroine whose life and adventures furnish the abundant materials of deep interest which form our present subject. Her qualities and virtues were severely tested and became publicly known. Her trials and endurances were many, and varied in kind.

The events of her life were frequently trying and remarkably chequered; and yet withal, she was gifted with the rare capacity and tact of adapting herself to any circumstances by which she was surrounded, or any events that might fall to her lot. She was a dutiful daughter, an affectionate wife, a prudent mother, an unchangeable friend, an amiable companion, and a sincere Christian. By those that knew her best, she was appreciated most, and perhaps by none more so than by Sir Alexander Macdonald of the Isles, and his talented lady, who treated her as if she had been their own child.

After an absence of such long duration from her native Isle, she appeared most anxious to procure a passage to the Long Island, to meet once more her brother at Milton and her friends at Ormiclade. On the last day of June, after remaining four days at Monkstadt, where she parted with her mother, she was favoured with a passage in a small sloop bound for Benbecula, where she landed in safety that evening. Her reception by Lady Clanranald, was a most cordial one, and her arrival was most heartily greeted by a numerous circle of relatives and friends. A large number of her old acquaintances, on receiving the intelligence of her return, assembled at Ormiclade to welcome her once more to her native place.

Poor Flora was quite bewildered by the enthusiastic reception which she met with from old and young, while the youthful associates of her early years claimed a preferable right to exhibit their fond congratulations and joy. Old Clanranald himself seemed extremely happy, and addressed his young friend in pure Gaelic:

Fhionnghail a' ghraidh, is mi 'tha toillichte do ghnuis shuairce fhaicinn a ris; is i do bheatha air ais chum eilein do bhreith, oir bha n fhardach gu'n aighear 's gu'n mhire o'n dh 'fhag thu I; agus bha eadhon 'Ceolag' fein, mar ri tuireadh, balbh.

Flora, my dear, I rejoice to see your comely face again. You are welcome back to the Isle of your birth, for the household was devoid of joy and gladness since you left it; and even 'Ceolag' itself (the small pianoforte), as if under lamentation, was mute.

At that time the excitement that pervaded the whole island, like most other parts of Scotland, was very great, on account of the rumours that the Young Chevalier was soon to visit them. The partisans of His Royal Highness from these quarters, who were along with him in France, especially Banker Macdonell, Kinlochmoidart's brother, held regular communications with their friends in the Isles and on the mainland, as to the movements and purposes of the prince.

The consequences were, that the different chiefs, and the most intelligent of their adherents and vassals, were in no small degree perplexed as to how they ought to act when the eventful crisis came to pass. Continued meetings were held among themselves, and trusty messengers were despatched to and fro from the Long Island to the mainland, and *vice versa*, to ascertain the intentions of all parties interested in the important affair. The claims of the prince to the throne of his forefathers were freely discussed, but were as freely condemned by some as they were approved by others. In this respect acrimonious differences arose betwixt chief and chief, brother and brother, father and son; and, hence, the confusion and perplexities that disturbed the peace of the country were, in every sense, great.

It was expected by the friends of the prince, as well as by himself, that the powerful chiefs, Sir Alexander Macdonald, and Macleod of Dunvegan, who could have raised more than a thousand men each, would have at once joined His Royal Highness, but both peremptorily declined. It can scarcely be said that the conduct of these chiefs was strictly honourable, as they promised their allegiance to the cause of the prince, on condition that he brought along with him a sufficient number of men and money, and munitions of war; but seeing that he failed in this, they considered themselves released from their engagement, and at once refused their aid.

While matters were thus going on, the intelligence spread rapidly far and near that the *Doutelle*, with the prince and retinue on board, had arrived at the Island of Eriska, in the Sound of Barra, on the 23rd day of July, 1745. Soon after casting anchor, the prince and most of his party landed on the Island, and were conducted to the house of "Aonghas Mac Dhomhnuill Mhic Sheumais," Angus Macdonald, tacksman of Eriska, where they passed the night. They were desirous of setting foot on *terra firma* after the fatigues of eighteen days at sea. As the prince did not at the time reveal himself to his hospitable landlord, whose knowledge of English was but scanty, he took him to be a chief attendant on the gentleman who had just landed from the frigate.

Unfortunately, the dwelling was so infested with smoke from the large peat fire in the middle of the chamber, that the prince frisked about, and went frequently outside the door for fresh air. The landlord was surprised, and perhaps a little offended at the stranger's restlessness, so that he called out, rather with an indignant smile, "Plague take that fellow! What is wrong with him, that he can neither sit nor stand still—neither can he keep within doors nor without doors."—*Jacobite Memoirs. Culloden Papers.*

The prince, eager to lose as little time as possible, made strict enquiry about old Clanranald, and other influential parties in the adja-

cent islands. He was informed that Clanranald was at home at Ormiclade; that his brother Alexander was at Boisdale; and that young
Clanranald was on the mainland at Moidart. He was aware that the
Clanranald branch of the Macdonalds was always favourable to the
cause of the Stuarts, and consequently he sent a messenger to Boisdale
wishing for an interview with him, believing that, as he was a man of
great prudence and sound judgment, he could prevail upon him to
secure the interest of the Clan at large, and especially so, that of his
brother the laird, and of his nephew, young Clanranald.

Boisdale appeared next morning on board the frigate; the interview took place, and it was everything but agreeable. The conversation
with the prince was firm and determined, and in all respects more
plain than pleasant. Boisdale told the prince that he had made up his
mind not to interfere further than earnestly to advise his brother and
nephew not to engage in such a hopeless and dangerous enterprise.
He further stated that Sir Alexander Macdonald and Macleod of Macleod were determined to stand aloof, and that under these circumstances, his best advice to His Royal Highness was to return at once to
France, and relinquish for ever such a foolish undertaking.

The prince was terribly annoyed at Boisdale's obduracy, but he
restrained his feelings, and appeared amiable and very agreeable. He,
however, exerted all his powers of eloquence, while the Doutelle was
weighing anchor, but Boisdale, whose boat was slung astern, listened
with patience, and after all, remained as inflexible as ever. When the
frigate had moved along for a mile or two under a gentle breeze, Boisdale leaped into his boat, and left His Royal Highness to ponder over
his great disappointment. Next day the *Doutelle* arrived safely at the
bay of Lochnanuagh, between Arasaig and Moidart.

The prince, sadly chagrined at the coldness and indifference of
Boisdale in not espousing his cause, sent a letter at once to young
Clanranald by Banker Macdonald, who went ashore, that his brother
Kinlochmoidart might accompany young Clanranald on board. They
were cheerfully welcomed by the prince, but in course of conversa-
tion young Clanranald enlarged upon the hopelessness of the adven-
ture, and the improbability of success, and was, in short, like his uncle
Boisdale, resolved not to interfere.

Charles, seeing that young Clanranald greatly sympathised with
him, and seemed to be warmly interested in his hopeless case, took
advantage of the young gentleman's feelings, and by his fawning, flattering, and agreeable talk, he received at length the assent of the young

chieftain to support his claims. The prince was as yet hopeful, not-withstanding Boisdale's declaration to the contrary, that Sir Alexander Macdonald and Macleod of Macleod would join him with their forces. Accordingly, he despatched young Clanranald and Mr. Allan Macdonald, a brother of Kinlochmoidart, to these chiefs with letters, earnestly soliciting their aid. Both chiefs replied to the message of His Royal Highness, that they considered his cause a desperate one, and that they would not engage in it.

The History of the Rebellion of 1745 is already well known. Within the compass of a few months an adventure came to a termination, on the fatal field of Culloden, which had but few parallels, if any, in the annals of history. When the expedition thus ended is viewed in its varied features and in the determination and boldness manifested in its several details, it may be considered to rank high among the achievements of ancient and modern times. The interests at stake were of the highest importance not only to the royal adventurer himself, but likewise to the different clans and septs that so imprudently espoused his cause.

What could be more hazardous than to rush with precipitation beyond the middle of England, and to traverse a hostile country to the very confines of the English Capital? As the talented Chambers has so well expressed it:

> The expedition was done in face of the two armies, each capable of utterly annihilating it; and the weather was such as to add a thousand personal miseries to the general evils of the campaign. A magnanimity was preserved even in retreat, beyond that of ordinary soldiers, and instead of flying in wild disorder, a prey to their pursuers, these desultory bands had turned against and smitten the superior army of their enemy with a rigour which effectually checked it. They had carried the standard of Glenfinnan a hundred and fifty miles into a country full of foes, and now they brought it back unscathed through the accumulated dangers of storm and war.

While the clans and country gentlemen—chieftains and their vassals—dukes and lords—and all ranks and classes in the Highlands and Lowlands, and over Scotland at large, viewed the adventure with the deepest anxiety, Miss Flora Macdonald experienced her own share of the general calamity. Personally she adhered to the loyal principles and feelings of her chief, Sir Alexander Macdonald, as well as of Old

Clanranald and his brother Boisdale. On the other hand, her amiable disposition in a sense compelled her to sympathise with the unfortunate prince under all his hardships and sufferings. She kept up a close correspondence with old friends and acquaintances in Edinburgh and elsewhere, and thereby became fully informed as to the various movements of that distinguished personage, whose life she was destined afterwards, under Providence, to preserve.

The family at Ormiclade, with whom Flora principally resided, were grievously perplexed at the aspect of existing events. Old Clanranald was night and day in deep distress, on account of the part which his son had taken in embracing the royal adventurer's cause, so directly in opposition to his father's will, and Lady Clanranald was nothing less so, but Flora, with her natural vivacity and geniality of temper, mightily soothed them in their grief. She assured them that they would be spared to see all going well. In due time the result of the Battle of Culloden became known in the Long Island, and created mixed feelings in the minds of the chief men of the place. To some the intelligence afforded no ordinary pleasure, while to others it created unbounded terror, under the dread that the ruling and now successful dynasty might inflict vengeance, and even the penalty of death, on those who had embraced the royal adventurer's cause. Such was the state of matters when the prince's last ray of hope was blasted for ever on the bloody field of Culloden.

By this time some of his movements became known to the government officials, and immediate steps were taken for his arrest, dead or alive. The intelligence of his arrival in the island created unprecedented commotion all over the Long Island. By this time, it became well known that "rebel hunting," as Cumberland and his lawless soldiery called it, was mercilessly practised in every quarter. It was too well known that the duke issued a proclamation denouncing immediate death, by being shot or hanged, against all persons who harboured any of the rebels, or aided them to escape into their mountain recesses. How much more so, were it possible, would the vengeance of these myrmidons of cruelty fall upon all and sundry who sheltered the prince himself.

Already about two thousand regular troops and militiamen were posted in suitable localities all over the island. Every avenue was guarded, every ferry had its watch, and every highway and hill-road was protected by soldiers. The lochs and bays, and the sea-coast all round, were so studded with sloops of war and cutters of all sizes, that no craft could possibly leave the island or come to it unknown, except perhaps under the dark shade of night. No two individuals could converse together on the highway without arousing the suspicion of some of the watching military.

The only consolation which the prince had cause to enjoy was the fact that he had many sincere friends on the island—possessed of prudence and caution, and ready to strain every nerve for his safety. Besides the friends who accompanied him from France, he had Clanranald, the proprietor of the island, Macdonald of Boisdale, the Macdonalds of Baileshear, and almost all the ladies of the island. Whether loyal or Jacobite, all united cordially in the wish that the royal fugitive would escape with his life from the island. Lady Clanranald and Miss Flora were continually engaged devising schemes for the immediate protection and ultimate release of the unfortunate prince, whom, however, as yet they had never seen.

Twelve powerful and trustworthy men, who could acquit themselves by sea or land, were selected by Lady Clanranald to be in readiness by night and day, should their services be required. Flora very frequently conversed with these gallant Islanders, and conveyed to them the sense she entertained of the responsible duties they might be called upon to perform. They had seen the prince on several occasions, but she had not. (The prince had a variety of places of concealment. Sometimes he hid himself in caves, and at other times in the lonely huts of shepherds or fishermen). One morning as two of them had come to Ormiclade to give intelligence as to how he had passed the night in his rocky cave, Flora met them at the door and asked them, "Am bheil e laghach? Am bheil e aoidheil? Am bheil e idir iriosal agus taitneach?" (Is he nice? Is he cheerful? Is he at all humble and pleasant?)

On another occasion she commenced, for her own amusement, to taunt them in a jocular manner, by telling them that she was able to direct them how to become far wealthier than Clanranald in less than a day's time.

"Oh! tell us, do tell us, how that can come to pass. More wealthy than our noble chief! Can such be really the case?"

"Oh, yes, perfectly true," said Flora with a smile, "and I will now tell you what means you are to use. Go immediately and give up the prince to my stepfather, Captain Hugh Macdonald, and as sure as the sun is now shining in the firmament, you shall have fifteen thousand pounds a piece for your great loyalty in doing so."

The answer was short, but decisive—"Nior leigeadh Ni Maith! Ochan! ged gheibheamaid an saoghal mu'n iadh a'ghrian, cha bhrathamaid ur n-oganach Rioghail gu brath" (Goodness forbid! Alas! should we receive the world around which the sun revolves, we would never betray our royal youth). Neither would they, nor any other Highlander then living; but it is to be feared, although the schoolmaster has long been abroad, that the same would not hold true today, (1882).

Clanranald, Boisdale, and their namesakes at Baileshear, with Lady Clanranald and Miss Flora, held a private council at Ormiclade, as to what must be done, and done immediately, seeing that every hour increased the danger to their unfortunate prince. It was resolved that he should be transported to Stornoway, as probably he might there receive the chance of a vessel to France. Donald Macleod of Galtrigal, the prince's faithful friend and pilot, was sent for, and all the preconcerted plans were explained to him. He acknowledged that the whole affair was pregnant with danger, but still agreed to execute his part of the scheme, if provided with a crew selected by himself, of which his own son Murdoch would be one.

★★★★★★

The history of Donald Macleod of Galtrigal is given in the *Celtic Magazine,* No. 19. Before the Battle of Culloden was fought, Murdoch, Galtrigal's son, was attending the Grammar School of Inverness, being then a youth of sixteen or seventeen. He understood that the battle was to be fought on a certain day, and on the morning of that day he left his school, procured a sword and dirk, and made for the battlefield. He stood there and fought for the prince, but received no wound. Hearing afterwards of the prince's wanderings in the West, he left Inverness, set off for Lochnanuagh, where he met his father, and assisted him in the dangerous voyage of conveying the prince and his friends from the main land to the Long Island.

★★★★★★

Seeing that longer delay was dangerous, the party set sail for Stornoway on the 29th of April, and Donald Macleod, knowing well the course to be taken, took his place at the helm. They had no sooner gone to sea, about midnight, than a severe storm arose, which, owing to the darkness of the night, placed them in no small danger, not only of being swamped, but of being dashed against the rocks or jutting headlands. The crew, however, bravely held on, under the direction of Donald Macleod, while two of them by turns kept constantly baling the boat, to prevent it from filling. About dawn they took shelter in a creek in the small Island of Glass, on the coast of Harris. (Glass is a little island on the coast of Harris, near the mouth of Loch Seafort, which divides Harris from Lewis. It is one of the stations selected many years ago for a lighthouse erected by the Commissioners of Northern Lights).

The tacksman of the island, Donald Campbell, to whom alone they made themselves known, treated them very kindly, and suggested that the prince should remain with him, while Macleod, the pilot, should visit Stornoway, to secure, if possible, a vessel to convey the royal fugitive to France. This plan was agreed upon, and after Macleod had reached the capital of the Lews, he thought that all would be right as he had secured a vessel for the intended purpose. His next step was to send a messenger immediately for the prince to the Island of Glass, as no time was to be lost. As the storm had not abated, sailing was impossible, and the royal fugitive had to walk through the trackless wilds of the Lews to the vicinity of Stornoway.

Unfortunately, one of Donald's crew got the worse of drink, and told his associates by way of boast that the hired vessel was intended to convey Prince Charles to France. In consequence of this unguarded announcement considerable alarm was created in the town, and all at once it was resolved that no vessel would be given on any conditions whatever, as such might involve the natives in serious trouble. It was then immediately decided by the prince and his associates to sail back to Benbecula in the face of any and every danger, and to trust once more to the schemes and contrivances of his friends there.

During his stay near Stornoway, the prince received shelter, and was kindly entertained at the house of Mrs. Mackenzie of Kildun at Arinish, about a mile from the village. Here His Royal Highness and friends spent many anxious hours in devising schemes, as to what they ought to do, the stormy deep preventing them from setting sail. Some of them, dreading immediate danger, proposed to betake themselves to the hills for concealment, but the prince objected, and suggested, if they did not make their way to Benbecula, that they should attempt to return to the mainland, in the hope of meeting with some vessel from France. Donald Macleod and the whole party, however, refused to entertain this hazardous plan, as their craft was too small, the voyage too long, and the danger of meeting with government vessels very great.

It was then agreed that they would leave Arinish before daybreak, and proceed southward along the coast of the Long Island. The morning was wet and somewhat stormy, but the wind was favourable, and they sailed along with great speed. At length they observed two ships against the horizon, evidently approaching them, and to avoid the danger of meeting them, they entered a creek in the small Island of Iffurt, a little north of the Island of Glass. Iffurt was occupied by a few fishermen, who, on observing the party, supposed them to be press-boat men, or a press-gang from some warship, and they consequently took to their heels at once, and concealed themselves among the rocks. Owing to the continued storm and other dangers, Charles and his friends remained four days on this island.

Next morning after their arrival they discovered the terrified fishermen, and assured them that they were quite safe. The poor men were overjoyed, and in return did everything in their power to show kindness to the strangers. They had abundance of fish and fuel, but their dwelling was a miserable hut, over which the prince's party spread the mainsail of their boat to exclude the rain.

On the 10th of May they left Iffurt and sailed for Glass. Finding, to their great disappointment, that their friend Donald Campbell had absconded under dread of being seized for entertaining the prince, they made no stay at Glass. They steered their course southward along the coast of Harris, but while crossing the mouth of Finsbay, they were observed by Captain Ferguson's war-ship which lay at the time in the bay. A well-manned boat was despatched, with all haste, in pursuit, but fortunately the fugitives escaped, having concealed themselves, in a small creek near Rodil, in Harris.

At nightfall they left their hiding-place, and sailed along the coast of North Uist, but when near Lochmaddy, another war-ship, which lay in the bay, observed them, and immediately set sail after them. The chase was hard and close; but fortunately the prince and his companions reached Benbecula, and just as they were getting ashore, the increasing storm, blowing off the land, drove the vessel of the enemy out to sea. To avoid seizure by the man-of-war, which was close in pursuit, they dashed their boat, under full sail, into a narrow creek, where the frail bark was splintered to fragments against the jutting rocks, leaving the prince and his companions floundering amid the foaming waves. They all however managed to reach dry land, whilst Charles cheerfully remarked to his friends that his escapes were marvellous, and that he believed in his heart that a kind Providence would permit him to be rescued in the end.

It has often been said that *truth is stranger than fiction*. This adage is perhaps in no instance more strikingly verified than in the case of the unfortunate Prince Charles Edward Stuart. His varied adventures, his critical dangers, his at times hopeful prospects, and his frequent hair-breadth escapes, are incidents in his daring career for which it is difficult to find a parallel in the history of any other man. One thing, however, is certain, that the cause of his having been rescued in the end arose not so much from any prudence or precaution on his own part as from friendly feelings secretly cherished by some of those employed by government to arrest him.

It is well known that great sympathy was felt for "Bonnie Prince Charlie," even by office-bearers of the Crown, all over the Highlands and Islands; and although some of these appeared outwardly to be actuated by no ordinary vigilance in discharging the duties of their mission, yet at heart they would be glad if he could effect his escape. Indeed, on several occasions they might have easily arrested him during his perilous wanderings in the Long Island if they had a mind to do so. It is true, on the other hand, that the captains and commanders of the frigates and sloops of war which scoured the creeks and coasts of the Western Isles were all in right earnest to capture him dead or alive. These however were generally confined to their own vessels at sea, and were consequently at considerable disadvantage in seizing their prey, who avoided going to sea, unless when compelled by necessity to do so.

In his perilous adventures from Stornoway to Benbecula he had to combat, not only with the violence of the elements, but likewise against the perpetual dread of being seized at any moment by some of the emissaries of the fleet of government vessels that sailed all around to capture him. By this time, it has been observed that on some occasions the unfortunate fugitive had become so heedless and hardened, and so much effected by despair, that he recklessly exposed himself to unnecessary dangers. No doubt the crisis as to his fate had become very critical, and matters looked as if they were very much beyond the power of his friends to devise means of effecting his rescue. On his arrival at Benbecula he and his faithful companions resorted, under the cover of night, to a small hut or hovel that lay a little distance, where they endeavoured to broil some shell-fish which they found among the rocks where they landed.

Next morning at break of day, the prince sent Donald Macleod to acquaint Clanranald of his arrival at Benbecula, and of the dangers by which he was beset. Donald related to the chief all dangers and difficulties which they had encountered in their fruitless voyage to Stornoway. Clanranald was much affected and deeply concerned with Donald's account of matters, thinking that by that time His Royal Highness had been safely transported to France. The worthy chief was sorely perplexed, and as he paced up and down the room he addressed the faithful Donald:

Och! a's och! a Dhomhnuill, the eagal mor orm, gu'm bheil grian Thearlaich, a bha aon uair co dealrach, gu dol fadha ann an uine ghearr ann an fuil, agus ann an tiugh-dhorchadas

(Alas! alas! Donald, I am greatly afraid that the sun of Charles, which was at one time so brilliant, is about soon to sink in blood and in darkness).

All this time Lady Clanranald sat silently in her armchair, sobbing and shedding tears. Flora was also present at this interview, and appeared spirited and cheerful. Turning round to Clanranald she smartly addressed him:

Tha do bhriathra ri Domhnull a' cur iongantais orm, oir fhad's a mhaireas beatha, mairidh dochas. Cuimhnich gu'm bheil an Ti Uile-bheannuichte sin a shuidhich ann an speuraibh neimhe a' ghrian ud a tha 'san am a' soillseachadh co dealrach, uile-chomusach air Tearlach a theasairginn o liontaibh a naimhdean

(I am astonished at your expressions to Donald, for while there is life there is hope. Remember that that ever Blessed Being who planted in the firmament of heaven yon sun which now shines so brightly is all-powerful to rescue Charles from the snares of his enemies).

Clanranald could not help smiling at his amiable *protégé's* confident remarks, and said:

O! Fhionghail, a' ghraidh, cha do chaill thu riamh do mhis-neach, agus tha dochas agam nach caill

(Oh! my dear Flora, you have never lost your courage, and I hope you never shall).

The interview ended by Clanranald sending the prince a message by Donald that he would visit him in his rude hiding-place without delay. After Donald's departure the chief became very impatient, and resolved to set off the same afternoon. In order not to appear at a distance from home without some apparent purpose, he equipped himself with all his shooting accoutrements, his gun, lead-belt and powder-flask, and started through the hills to the place of concealment. At the same time Niel MacEachainn, who generally resided at Ormiclade, was to resort that same evening to the prince's hovel, with a supply of shirts, shoes, and stockings, and a quantity of brandy and wine, to contribute to the scanty comforts of His Royal Highness.

Niel MacEachainn (Niel, the son of Hector Macdonald) was a faithful inmate at Ormiclade, being an intelligent, smart Jack-of-all-trades. He was a pretty well educated youth and made himself generally useful about the place. He had spent several years in Paris, whither he was taken when a mere boy by Banker Macdonald as body-servant. He learned to speak the French language fluently, and was therefore a very suitable messenger to send to the prince, as he could talk in that language to His Royal Highness unintelligibly to all around him.

★★★★★★

Niel was a descendant of the Macdonalds of Howbeag, in South Uist, where he was born, and having followed the prince to France, he became the father of the celebrated Marshal Macdonald, Duke of Tarentum, one of Napoleon's most distinguished generals. The Macdonalds of Howbeag were a distinct, secluded sept of that clan, who had not been, for some cause, very much esteemed by the generality of their neighbours.

★★★★★★

When Clanranald arrived at the prince's hovel he was shocked at its miserable state, and he prevailed on His Royal Highness to leave it as soon as possible, and remove to a more comfortable retreat in the hill of Corrodale. Meantime the prince falling short of means, despatched his trusty friend, Donald Macleod, with letters to General Murray, and Lochiel, craving a supply of money without delay. Macleod accidentally met these gentlemen at the head of Loch Arkaig, in Lochaber, where they gave him a written reply to the prince expressing regret that they had no money to send him.

The new residence of the fugitive was the Forest-house of Glencorrodale, and although in a very lonely, sequestered place, he found it more comfortable and suitable than his last miserable abode. While it was dismally gloomy, and deeply-buried in the Corrodale hills, yet it had one great advantage, that its situation afforded recreation to His Royal Highness. The forest abounded in game of all kinds, abundance of grouse and deer, and the prince possessed great dexterity in the use of his gun. But he used it at times very incautiously. One afternoon, he and two of his faithful adherents went to the moor, expecting to succeed in shooting a roe or a deer.

After the prince had fired at some grouse that came in his way, he observed, to his horror, a small band of militia upon the shoulder of the hill, at a very little distance from him; whereupon he had no alternative but to run and conceal himself in a ravine close by, and to give his gun to one of his attendants, with instructions to go heedlessly forward in the direction of the soldiers, and, should they meet them on the heights, to appear in their presence as if nothing were amiss. It was afterwards ascertained that the militia was commanded by Captain Hugh Macdonald, Flora's stepfather, who was at the time well aware that the prince was one of the shooting party, but, being a Jacobite at heart, Hugh had no desire to capture the prince.

On several other occasions Charles had very narrow escapes from the troops of militia in the island. One evening, under the impression that there was no danger, he went off a little distance from the shore, in a small boat, to fish for lythe, and took Niel MacEachainn and one or two more of his attendants along with him. The prince was dressed in a rough greatcoat and broad Highland bonnet; such as were usually worn at the time by the common people of the place. Fishing for lythe requires the boat to be smartly and continuously rowed, having hand-lines and hooks baited with red or white pieces of cloth attached to them, and let out from the stern of the boat.

While thus busily employed, a party of red-coats appeared on the elevated cliff overhanging the sea-beach, observing the boat at sea, about half a mile from the shore. They fired a shot, whereupon the boatmen stood up and waved their bonnets over their heads, loudly shouting, "Hurrah! Hurrah!" The soldiers, observing such want of concern on the part of the crew, took them to be some of the peasantry, turned right about, and immediately departed.

The prince was made fully aware of his dangerous position, and of the public opinion of friends and foes in the nation at large, regarding his perilous movements and prospects. Lady Margaret Macdonald, who was fervently attached to his interests, regularly sent him the newspapers of the day, through Baileshear, who, though himself a captain of one of the companies of militia raised to suppress the rebellion, was at heart friendly to the prince, and even visited him with Boisdale at Glen-Corrodale. The newspapers thus sent by Lady Margaret were the *Edinburgh Evening Courant*, the *Caledonian Mercury*, and the *Glasgow Journal*, said to have been the only newspapers of importance in

Scotland at that period.

★★★★★★

It would seem that the *Glasgow Journal* was a loyal print, and adverse to the cause of the rebels, but in order to be revenged on the politics of that journal, they destroyed its printing press, types &c. There can be no doubt that the proprietors of the *Journal* are among the sufferers alluded to in the following paragraph in the *Caledonian Mercury* of the 10th January, 1746:—

> The rebels carried off from Glasgow a printing press, types, and other materials for that business (printing Prince Charles' declarations, &c), together with servants to work in that way. When they carried off these materials they did it in this way— that is, from one printer they took a press, from another some types, and from a third chases, furniture, frames, &c. This happened when the insurgents were on their final retreat northward, after their madly undertaken, and as madly abandoned, incursion into England.

★★★★★★

As day after day passed, matters were becoming more critical and dangerous for the safety of the prince. The government authorities became aware that he was unquestionably in concealment in South Uist or Benbecula, and they issued strict orders to surround these islands with sloops of war, and carefully to guard every creek, loch, and bay, to prevent any possibility of escape. Besides these guardian vessels, additional companies of militia and regular soldiers were landed in the Long Island, to search the hills and dales, and to prevent any sailing craft of any size to go to sea until they had searched and ransacked, not only the crews individually, but all their bunkers and recesses.

All this was done to prevent the concealment of papers or letters going to friends in any quarter that might suggest plans for effecting the rescue of the prince. Lady Margaret in Skye became fully aware of the measures taken in the Long Island to seize upon the eagerly sought-after prize; but her ladyship was doubtful whether the prince himself had been apprised of the real danger in which he stood, and consequently she sent a verbal communication to Baileshear, by the master of a sloop sailing for Benbecula, pressing upon him to see the prince, and to make everything known to him. As soon as opportunity offered, Baileshear, with his friend Boisdale, went at night to Glencorrodale and had an interview with the prince, who rejoiced to see them, and who treated them with hearty Highland hospitality.

The prince, deeply grateful to Lady Margaret for her great interest in him, wrote her a kind letter of thanks, which he handed to Baileshear for transmission. Baileshear at the same time told him that the master of the sloop who conveyed Lady Margaret's verbal message to him was returning to Skye in a day or two with a number of young cattle, and that he would contrive to send the letter by him. To avoid detection, Baileshear enclosed it in one from himself to his brother, Captain Donald Roy Macdonald, who resided at the time with Sir Alexander Macdonald, at Monkstadt. Captain Macdonald was lame at the time, in consequence of a musket ball having gone through his left foot at Culloden, and of his having walked in great pain all the way to Skye to receive treatment from a celebrated local surgeon, Dr. Maclean, at Shulista, near Monkstadt. On his arrival in Skye from the battlefield he had the prudence to surrender his arms to Captain Macleod of Balmeanach, who allowed him his freedom, though afterwards he was made prisoner as a rebel.

Baileshear gave strict injunctions to his brother to see that his own letter and that of the prince to Lady Margaret were consigned to the flames when read. This was done to the great regret of her ladyship afterwards. Baileshear pointed out in his letter that the prince would require without delay to leave the Long Island, and that probably he would be landed on the small island of Fladda-Chuain, on the north coast of Troternish; but this was not the case. Baileshear was much perplexed as to how he would secure the letters from the searching of the harpies who were sure to ransack every hole and corner of the cattle-ship.

A little before that time a vessel had been wrecked on the coast of South Uist, which had been laden with a mixed cargo; and among other things several casks of coffee beans had drifted ashore and were sold for trifling prices to the natives. Baileshear filled one of these small barrels with beans, and placed his letter in the bottom of the cask. He then covered the whole with a suitable lid, and addressed it to his brother in Skye. The captain was instructed to tell, on delivering the cask, where the letter would be found. This done, the craft was ready to set sail, but no sooner had the government officials observed that preparations were being made for departing than they went on board and diligently searched the crew and all the keeping-places in the vessel. Even the lid of the barrel which contained the letter was lifted, when they found it full to the brim with beans of coffee. All was found right, and they leaped ashore.

A few days after this the prince came to understand that Boisdale and his own faithful adherent, Donald Macleod of Galtrigal, were taken prisoners, and this intelligence sadly grieved him. Dreading that his quarters at Glen-Corrodale had been made known to the government spies, he left the place under cover of night with Captain O'Neal, and went to a more concealed retreat in Benbecula. By this time the whole country was in a state of great excitement and alarm. Night after night Ormiclade was crowded with the friends of the prince, in order if possible to devise some plan for his escape. Clanranald did not think his present place of concealment at all safe, hence the necessity of having him removed at once from his hut, and getting him concealed in some natural cave still more difficult of access, until, if at all within the range of possibility, he might be conveyed from the island.

Captain O'Neal, the faithful companion and friend of the prince, along with Baileshear and others, waited one evening upon the laird, at Ormiclade, for the purpose of adopting some prompt measures for the immediate rescue of the fugitive, as the danger was alarmingly increasing. Several plans were proposed, but each had some insurmountable difficulty. At length Lady Clanranald addressed herself to Flora Macdonald, who sat silently and pensively in a corner of the room, and solicited her aid, as well as the exercise of her ingenuity, for the relief of the unfortunate stranger. Flora still sat in deep meditation, and uttered not a word.

"Flora, dear," said her ladyship, "just consider for a moment the dignity, the honour, the glory, of saving the life of your lawful prince!"

"My dear lady," responded Flora, "the matter is difficult, perplexing, and dangerous, and it might be ruinous to all to plunge too precipitately into any scheme without pondering over it in all its bearings."

"All true, my dear Flora, but we all know that you are the only person, in this trying emergency, whom we deem at all likely to be able to effect the rescue, if you have the moral courage to attempt it."

"Moral courage!" retorted Flora, as if hurt by the reflection. "Moral courage! Ah! yes, my dear Lady Clanranald, moral courage will never fail me, never; yet still moral courage may not be able to work impossibilities. I care not to endanger, or even sacrifice my valueless life, if I can but see my way to save the valuable life of the unfortunate prince. As yet, however, the prospects are to me dark and gloomy."

It was a moment of great suspense to every member of the friendly circle on that eventful evening at Ormiclade, but not so much so to any as to the gallant Flora. She possessed abilities superior to anything like ostentation; while she was influenced by goodness of heart that was quite satisfied with its own reward. She was blessed with a sound, discriminating judgment, which braced her to discharge what she considered important duties. It was now, however, that the prudence, firmness, and devotedness of the young heroine's well-balanced mind were severely put to the test. She had to decide at once against the influence of three conflicting elements, all important in themselves. She had to brave the danger of the doubtful enterprise.

She had to run the risk of entailing ruin and disgrace upon her chief, Sir Alexander Macdonald, and his Lady, and she had to meet the strong and perhaps reasonable objections to her hazardous undertaking by her only living brother, whom she dearly loved. No doubt poor Flora was at the moment in a very perplexing dilemma. Those around her placed all confidence in her, as a smart, intelligent young woman of excellent address and prudence; and they encouraged her by the assurance that her stepfather, Captain Hugh Macdonald, who then commanded a detachment of the militia, and who retained a warm feeling at heart towards the Stuarts, would at once procure for her a passport under his own hand to enable her to leave the Long Island.

Flora listened calmly to all these remarks, and for some time made no reply. Lady Clanranald again addressed her, and urgently solicited that she would express her mind as to the important proposals which had been made to her. Flora answered:

Indeed, my dear Lady, I have come to the conclusion that the chances of success are extremely small. I am really of opinion that the escape of the prince to Skye is almost impossible, and I will state my reasons. You know well, my dear Lady, that the Macdonald, Macleod, and Campbell Militia are just now commanding every pass and creek. Then it is certain that the prince is well known to all these to be on this island. It is publicly announced that thirty thousand pounds are set as a price upon his head. And further, we are too well aware that the white sails of England are presently scouring over Loch Skiport, Loch Boisdale, and the other friths around us, so that, in my humble view, a sparrow cannot escape without their knowledge and consent. But think not, dear Lady, for a moment that I consider my own personal danger. Certainly not, for I am ready and willing at any hour to peril my life, and to sacrifice everything personal to myself to forward the enterprise, if you think that there is even a shadow of success. My only dread is not for myself, but for the ruin that may be entailed upon my noble friend, Sir Alexander Macdonald, if I succeed in conveying the royal fugitive to his estates in Skye.

All present felt greatly relieved by this announcement from the lips of their young and gallant friend, who seemed to be heedless of personal danger, and to be inspired with a spirit resembling that of Esther of old when she said—"If I perish, I perish."

Like most others in the Highlands at the time, Flora herself felt a very deep and friendly personal interest in the welfare of the prince, not on political grounds so much as from motives of pure compassion for suffering humanity. As yet she had never seen him, but she cherished the greatest sympathy for his varied privations and severe hardships.

In *Waverley* Sir Walter Scott has beautifully delineated the general traits of Flora's character, and her loyalty to the House of Stuart— at least to this royal aspirant to the British throne under his misfortunes—is represented as the ruling passion of her youthful, generous heart. Well then may we fancy that on hearing the news of the landing of Prince Charles in Scotland, and his raising of the Royal Standard on the hills of Moidart; and when he called on the chiefs of Macdonald, Lochiel, and Glengarry to uphold that banner, the enthusiastic Flora would breathe in silent aspiration the well-known lines:—

Up with the banner,
Let the forest winds fan her,
It has waved o'er the Stuarts ten ages and more;
In sport well attend her,
In battle defend her,
With hearts and with hands like our fathers before.

Matters were now hastening to a crisis. Each successive day added to the intensity of danger to the unfortunate Charles. It was not without many hair-breadth escapes and many striking exhibitions of loyalty on the part of his steadfast friends, that he was hitherto preserved from his vigilant pursuers. For several weeks the search for him was rendered more vigorous by its being known to his enemies that he was within the narrow bounds of a comparatively small island. As has been said, the possibility of his escape, according to Miss Flora's shrewd opinion, might be considered miraculous, or at all events marvellous. It will ever be recorded to the honour of the Highlanders that out of the host of persons, mostly of inferior station in life, with whom he came in contact, not one was tempted by the great bribe offered to betray him.

At Ormiclade another large meeting of friends was held at night, to mature the plans and preparations to be immediately resorted to for the hazardous adventure. Lady Clanranald stated that she for one was entirely disposed to be guided by Flora's suggestions, as she had agreed to become the heroine of the dangerous enterprise. Flora said but little, yet with the air of a calm but independent spirit we can easily imagine her illustrating the sentiment of Smollett's beautiful ode,—

Thy spirit, Independence, let me share,
Lord of the Lion heart, and Eagle eye,
And I will follow with my bosom bare,
Nor heed the storm that howls along the sky.

The whole party greatly admired her conduct, and complimented her upon the judiciousness of her plans, all agreeing, however, that they must be acted upon with every possible expedition. She was no doubt greatly influenced by the principles of sympathy and pure humanity in contributing to the safety of the prince apart altogether from political views. She had now learned all about his miserable state; the cold, damp cave in which he had taken refuge; his gaunt, haggard, and half-famished appearance; his clothes in tatters from his solitary wanderings for so many weeks amid the caves and recesses of those sterile mountains. At these her woman's heart relented. The pure sympathy of her nature yielded to the pressure of the demand now made upon her. A spirit of romantic chivalry overcame every other consideration, and with a sublime heroism worthy of the blood of Clanranald, she declared her readiness to act, and to die if need be in the attempt to save her prince!

Clanranald and his Lady, Captain O'Neal, Baileshear, and others at Ormiclade, began to arrange their plans that they might soon be put into execution. Milton, Flora's brother, although one of the friends of the prince, was not at Ormiclade on this important occasion. He at first intended to have been there, but now pleaded indisposition as an excuse for his absence. It was, however, well known that he was a prudent, cautious man, and, although desiring that all would fare well with the prince, he had no wish to be involved in what he considered the perilous schemes now to be devised for his release. Milton wanted much of the determination and magnanimity of his sister, yet he was much respected for his integrity and sterling honesty.

On the next evening after the meeting at Ormiclade, Flora resolved to go to Milton and acquaint her brother of all that had been done, and more especially to intimate to him the dangerous and difficult part which was allotted to herself in the enterprise. She was well aware that she would meet with his stern opposition to the very risky duties that she had undertaken to perform. Indeed, she said to Lady Clanranald that, in a sense, she had a greater dread of meeting the expected disapproval of her dear and only brother than she had to face the many perils to which the whole enterprise was exposed.

On her arrival at Milton she met her brother near the house, and at once observed, pictured in his visage, the great displeasure that evidently rankled in his heart. He addressed her sternly saying:

What is this you are about to do, my foolish sister? Are you recklessly to submit to be made a tool of in a scheme that is, as sure as death, to terminate in ruin to yourself, to our kindred, country, and clan? Can you not see that failure in the enterprise, which will be the more probable result by far, may subject all who take a part in it to the punishment of imprisonment and death? Just consider what Cumberland has already done by fire, and sword, and death, on the mainland; and can you, silly woman, expect to receive more mercy at his cruel hands, if found out as one of the prominent protectors of his great but unfortunate rival, Prince Charles Edward Stuart.

Flora listened patiently to this painful address, marked all her brother's expressions with earnest attention, but remained inexorable. After a few moments of calm reflection, and when she had observed that his feelings had somewhat subsided, she addressed him:

My dear Angus, do you not believe that there is an over-ruling Providence, and a benevolent Being who has the control of all events? Take matters easy, my dear brother, and do not concern yourself about me. It will be all right, for God will prosper the adventure.

Flora spent the night at Milton, and remained until the evening of the following day, when she set off along with her servant, Niel MacEachainn, for Ormiclade. As she had not been furnished with a passport from any of the militia officers, she resolved to travel at night, expecting to reach her destination in safety. In this, however, she was sadly disappointed, for in passing one of the fords on her way to Clanranald's mansion, she and her attendant, the faithful MacEachainn, were pounced upon by a party of Major Allan Macdonald's company, and detained prisoners for the night.

Major Allan was one of the most inveterate and cruel officers in the whole service against the adherents of the prince, as will be afterwards shewn. Flora felt very uncomfortable, dreading that she might be detained as a prisoner, and that in consequence her intended services to rescue the prince might prove abortive. She ventured to ask one of those in the guardhouse who the officer in command was, and when he would appear there? She was informed that Captain Hugh Macdonald was in command and that he was expected to be there in the morning at an early hour. This intelligence at once dissipated the fears under which she had for some hours suffered.

On the arrival of the captain, he was surprised to find his stepdaughter in the guard-house, a small turf-built hut, roofed with bulrushes. A long conversation took place between them in private, in which, no doubt, they fully discussed all the schemes and plans that were to be resorted to to secure the preservation of the prince. The captain cherished the most friendly feelings towards His Royal Highness, and it was undoubtedly the desire of his heart that he might escape. Had the captain been half as vigilant and inveterate as his Skye countryman and neighbour, Major Allan Macdonald of Knock, Charles would long before then have fallen into the relentless hands of his enemies.

Flora, in the hearing of the military present, subsequently addressed her stepfather and informed him that she had a strong desire to go to Skye and visit her mother at Armadale, to avoid all these unpleasant encounters with the soldiers, who then ransacked every dwelling, and creek, and corner of the Long Island. To this natural request the captain readily assented, and promised to transmit to her by a trusty messenger that evening the necessary passports for herself, her man-servant (Niel MacEachainn), an Irish spinning-maid, named Betty Burke, and for six of a crew. It is needless to say that Betty Burke the smart Irish girl, was none else than Prince Charles Stuart. Late at night the passports were handed to Flora at Ormiclade by a sergeant of Captain Macdonald's company. In addition to the passports the good captain addressed a letter to his wife (Flora's mother), written on an unsealed sheet of paper and framed in the following terms:—

My Dear Marion,—I have sent your daughter from this country, lest she should be any way frightened with the troops lying here. She has got one Betty Burke, an Irish girl, who, as she tells me, is a good spinster. If her spinning please you, you can keep her till she spin all your lint; or, if you have any wool to spin, you may employ her. I have sent Niel MacEachainn along with your daughter and Betty Burke, to take care of them.—I am, your dutiful husband,

Hugh Macdonald.

June, 22nd 1746.

★★★★★★

About forty-five years ago, (as of 1882), this letter was seen by the writer in the careful possession of Miss Mary Macleod, of Stein, in Skye. Miss Macleod was a grand-daughter of Flora Macdonald. She had a variety of relics that belonged to the prince, such as rings, lockets, an ivory miniature likeness of himself, and other ornaments in gold and silver.

★★★★★★

Finding that the gallant heroine was now fortified with passports and plans, a number of friends met privately at Ormiclade, who with the Laird and his Lady were to lose no time in making every necessary and suitable arrangement. It was an evening of the deepest anxiety to all present, as the fate of the prince depended solely on the scheme to be resorted to that night. Of all the preparations being made in his interest the unfortunate fugitive himself knew little or nothing except perhaps a general idea that may have been conveyed to him by Captain O'Neal, who visited him as often as possible.

As the hut in which Charles had been hitherto concealed was within a short distance of a military station, he deemed it prudent to shift his quarters to Rossinish, in doing which he and O'Neal nearly lost their lives. They were ignorant as to the nature of the journey, and owing to the darkness of the night, they had almost fallen over a precipice. O'Neal lost no time in acquainting his friends at Ormiclade of the prince's new place of concealment; and in return he was instructed to acquaint His Royal Highness that all preparations were now matured, and would speedily be put into execution.

An excellent six-oared boat, the best that could be had, and six stalwart and experienced seamen, were already selected and secured, and sworn-in to be faithful. These were in readiness to attend orders, and to meet the party at a fixed time and place. A great portion of the evening was spent in procuring from Lady Clanranald's wardrobe suitable habiliments for the poor, ragged Irish girl. The difficulty experienced was not from any scarcity of every variety of garments in the good Lady's possession, but from the uncommonly awkward, masculine-like stature of that half-famished maiden! Whether or not she had been fed, like many of her benighted countrymen, on "potatoes and point," is open to doubt, but whatever had been her nourishment, she exhibited such an enormous size for a young peasant female that article after article, as produced by the good Lady of Ormiclade, was cast aside by the unanimous verdict of the company as ridiculously small.

However, the dress finally condescended upon was one almost entirely made up that same evening by all who could handle a needle in the house. It consisted of a flowered linen gown, sprigged with blue, a light-coloured quilted petticoat, a large cap, and broad apron, and a mantle of grey-coloured camlet with a large hood, such as Irish girls were in the habit of wearing. Next day being the 26th of June, when everything was carefully prepared, Lady Clanranald, Flora, and Niel MacEachainn, the latter of whom carried Betty Burke's dress in a well-packed bundle, were cautiously conducted by O'Neal to the miserable abode where the prince was concealed, seven or eight miles distant from the mansion-house of Ormiclade.

At length they arrived in safety, and found His Royal Highness alone at the time in his wretched cave. The elegant youth, the descendant of a line of kings stretching back to the remotest antiquity, was here found roasting kidneys and the heart and liver of a sheep for his humble repast. The sight, which was most affecting, moved the party to tears; but the natural, cheerful, and affable demeanour of the prince soon restored his affected visitors to calm composure of mind. At his request, they all sat down to partake of his cookery.

The table was a flat stone resting on a pillar of turf, while the seats on which they sat were bundles of heather closely packed and tied together. Though the fare consisted of no great variety, yet it was very substantially supplemented by a large supply of prepared meat and roasted fowls, as well as by an abundance of wine, brandy, and other acceptable eatables and viands that had just arrived from Ormiclade, as requisites for the intended voyage. While thus seated at his primitive and rude table, the prince greatly amused his guests by racy anecdotes and facetious remarks. Indeed, he made himself so agreeable that all present were charmed with his affability and pleasant manners.

It may be stated that this was the first time Flora had ever seen him whom all along she was so very eager to rescue. Although the prince had been for such a long time a hunted fugitive on that island, yet Flora studiously avoided meeting him until that evening. Clanranald and his Lady had seen him frequently, and did all in their power to contribute to his comforts, but Flora, quite contrary to the general impression, had never had a sight of him, until Lady Clanranald had introduced her to him that night, as the young lady who was ready to sacrifice her life for his safety.

Probably Flora's great precaution and prudence were the motives which prevented her from visiting the prince earlier. She no doubt desired to keep herself clearly aloof from an interview, as in the event of her intentions to rescue him being discovered by his pursuers, she could truthfully plead in defence the unreasonableness of accusing her of favouring a person whom she had never seen, and of whom she personally knew nothing.

When the homely royal repast was over, Lady Clanranald suggested that it was now time to begin the business for which they had met, and to get the prince robed in his new habiliments. To the no small amusement of all present, Flora unloosed the parcel, and produced the newly made-up antique dress of Betty Burke. She explained to the prince that he must now assume the character of that Irish spinning-maid, to suit the passport which she had procured for him. He laughed heartily at the idea, though he had previously been furnished by O'Neal with some description of his new dress. Yet on seeing the reality he could not restrain his risible faculties, though he greatly appreciated the ingenuity of the contrivance, thanked Flora for it in the kindest terms, and expressed a hope that her plans would be attended with success.

His Royal Highness then retired with O'Neal to the cleft of a rock in the neighbourhood to get robed in his new vestments. After an absence of twenty minutes he returned, when to the no small merriment of the ladies, he stood before them as a tall, awkward, Irish servant. Scarcely had the metamorphosis been completed than a private messenger arrived, announcing that Captain Ferguson and Major Allan Macdonald, with troops of soldiers, had reached Ormiclade, and that in consequence it was absolutely necessary that Lady Clanranald should hasten home to avoid suspicion. She accordingly took an affectionate leave of the prince, and left the heroic Flora, Captain O'Neal, and Niel MacEachainn to pass the night with him.

It was now a period of indescribable anxiety, yet the soul of Flora felt no fear. She rose superior to the dire emergency of that eventful evening, and in none of the trying scenes of her chequered life does she appear to more advantage than in her firmness and mental determination that night, in that cave, in the presence of the prince and his friends, after the departure of Lady Clanranald. Captain O'Neal, who had been the inseparable companion of His Royal Highness, insisted on accompanying him from the island, while the prince, in turn, refused to be separated from his faithful friend.

At this juncture Flora addressed the prince, and told him in a firm, determined tone of voice, that his proposal to Captain O'Neal was utterly and clearly impracticable! She spoke respectfully, but very decidedly, and her demeanour on this occasion showed the natural inflexibility of her will as well as the sagacity of her judgment.

Your Royal Highness must at once understand that as I procured passports for three persons only; that is, one each for myself and my servant, and one for my mother's spinning-maid, the attempt of a fourth to escape without a passport, and especially so Captain O'Neal, a gentleman so well known to every officer and soldier all over the island, would jeopardise the lives of us all.

To this firm and conclusive reasoning the prince and O'Neal yielded at once, although, no doubt, with considerable reluctance. About midnight Flora, Captain O'Neal, and Niel MacEachainn took leave of the prince, and left him to meditate in his lonely solitude. Flora made the best of her way to bid farewell to her brother, as the coming evening was the one appointed for the attempt to get across to Skye. Captain O'Neal was that morning arrested by a party of the military on his way to Ormiclade, and made prisoner.

When Lady Clanranald had arrived at her own home she was rigidly and even rudely questioned by General Campbell and Captain Ferguson, who insisted on her telling them where she had been, when she left home, and what was the cause of her absence? She replied, with firm composure, that she had a very good reason for her absence, and one that caused her much grief; that she was visiting a dear dying friend. And it was true that she did call on her way home upon a young lady suffering in the last stages of a rapid consumption.

About ten o'clock at night the following evening, being Friday, the 27th June, 1746, the prince, Flora, and Niel MacEachainn proceeded to the sea-shore, to the place where it was previously arranged they should meet the boat. On their arrival, wet and weary, as the rain fell in torrents, they observed to their horror several small vessels or wherries, filled with armed men, sailing within a gunshot of the spot where they lay concealed. Fortunately, however, these objects of terror tacked in an opposite direction, and soon disappeared in the hazy gloom. In about an hour after, their own boat, which lay concealed in a neighbouring creek, rowed up gently with muffled oars to the spot where they were so anxiously awaiting it. With all possible speed they embarked on their perilous voyage across the Minch to Skye, a distance of between thirty-five and forty miles.

The prince was more anxious to get to Skye than any quarter on the mainland, as that island was almost entirely the property of two clans, the Macdonalds and Macleods, both of whom were ostensibly hostile to the Jacobite cause. On this account Cumberland had sent but few of his government troops to occupy that island, and to set a watch upon the movements of strangers. Charles was likewise well aware that he had a warm and faithful friend in Lady Margaret, the wife of Sir Alexander Macdonald of Sleat, whose kindness His Royal Highness had already experienced.

The voyage was perilous in the extreme, as the whole channel was scoured by government vessels, eager to arrest the prince dead or alive, and also seeing that the chances for eluding their grasp were exceedingly small. It was with them, however, now *to do or die*, and the attempt had to be made. At first the breeze was moderate and favourable, but in a few hours one of those sudden summer storms, so common in those Isles unexpectedly came on. The wind blew in terrific gusts, the billows rolled mountains high, threatening to engulph their small craft. To make matters worse, one of those thunder-storms with which the Hebrideans are so familiar set in, and at one time the party became painfully alarmed as to their safety. Their boat was an open one, about twenty-four feet keel, but one of the best that the Long Island could furnish.

The crew were sturdy, well-picked men, and excellent seamen, well skilled in managing their craft in a storm, and yet that night they had much to do. Their utmost energies were called forth to manage their boat amid the raging billows. They had no compass, and when less than two hours at sea, the storm increased to such a terrific degree, that the ocean was lashed into deep, foaming waves! At that moment, as if to add to their already indescribable terror, thunder rolled in rattling peals over their heads, while the lightning flashed from cloud to cloud in the murky atmosphere! The crew had to steer before the wind, which frequently shifted, and for hours they were entirely at the mercy of the raging elements. Yet they did their work calmly and steadily, though at times they instinctively exclaimed to one another—"Ochan! is ochan! is e tha gàrbh! is e tha gàrbh." "Alas! alas; it is rough; it is rough"—and so it was.

The prince all along behaved nobly. He cheered and animated the seamen by relating anecdotes, but chiefly by singing verses of sea-songs. Poor Flora, anxious and fatigued, and no doubt alive to the many dangers that surrounded her, became overpowered with sleep. She lay on the ballast of the boat wrapped in a plaid, and the prince kept watch to prevent her slumbers from being disturbed. At break of day they were greatly perplexed at seeing no land in any direction—nothing visible but the azure horizon all round, and without a compass they did not know how to direct their craft. The storm had by this time fortunately moderated, and while the seamen had been steering at random for so many hours, their hearts were at last cheered, by beholding in the dim distance the lofty headlands of Skye.

They made speedily for the shore, and soon approached the Point of Waternish, a promontory on the north-west coast of that island. But who can judge of their dismay, when, on drawing near the land, they beheld a large party of the Macleod Militia on the beach waiting their arrival! The crew immediately cried with one simultaneous shout—"Mach i! Mach i! Mach i! air ball!"—"Out with her! Out with her! to sea with her immediately!"—and with a few desperate pulls the boat was soon rowed beyond the reach of the red-coats on shore.

The militia, sadly disappointed, and having no boat fit to pursue, fired a shower of bullets after them, which fortunately did no injury, though the balls struck and riddled their sails. The danger was indeed great, for one of the balls cleft the handle of the helm, and grazed one of the steerman's fingers, but did no further injury. The prince stood up and cheered the crew, and told them not to mind the fellows ashore, but to continue doing their duty as they had hitherto so bravely done.

During the rapid firing of the militia, he was endeavouring to persuade Flora to recline in the bottom of the boat; but the heroine, with a generosity of soul that stamped her among the bravest of her sex, refused, unless the prince himself, whose life she considered far more valuable than her own, would take the same precaution. Eventually as the danger increased, and as the bullets whizzed past close to their ears, the prince, Flora, and Niel squatted down all three on the ballast flags, and continued in that position until the boat had receded beyond the reach of danger.

Early on the afternoon of Saturday they landed safely at a place called Kilbride, in the parish of Kilmuir, and within five hundred yards of the house of Monkstadt, the residence of Sir Alexander Macdonald of the Isles.

CAVE IN SKYE OCCUPIED BY PRINCE
CHARLES JUST BEFORE LEAVING FOR RAASAY

CHAPTER 5

Flora and the Prince in the Isle of Skye—From Kingsburgh to Portree

There was at this time a small cave under a shelving rock at Kilbride, which was beyond the high-water mark, and the prince took shelter in it, making a seat of Flora's trunk, which was carried from the boat for that purpose. This cave has since been demolished by the removal of stones from it for building purposes. After the prince, Flora, and the faithful Niel, had been safely landed, the crew rowed the boat into an adjoining creek, where they expected to have enjoyed some rest, and to partake of the abundance of refreshments which they had with them, all along, but which, owing to the storm, they were unable to touch since they had left the Long Island the night before. Flora, accompanied by her servant Niel, walked at once to Monkstadt House, while, for a short time the prince was alone in his solitary cave.

> 'Tis midnight: a lone boat is on the sea,
> And dark clouds gather, but no thoughts of fear
> Chill those brave hearts! A princely refugee
> Disguised—a faithful maiden sitting near,
> Upon whose cheek anon there falls a tear—
> Fond woman's pledge of sympathy. A crew,
> Trusty and gallant, labour at the oars.
> The shifting wind white showers of spray uprears
> Like incense heavenward; the water roars,
> While from huge murky clouds the lurid lightning pours!

Sir Alexander Macdonald was fortunately from home at this time, otherwise his presence might have been a painful circumstance to himself, as well as a restraint upon the humanity and benevolence

DUNVEGAN CASTLE, SKYE, 1772

of his Lady, a staunch Jacobite at heart, while Sir Alexander himself refused to support the cause of the prince. The worthy baronet was then at Fort-Augustus in attendance upon the Duke of Cumberland, who was at the time engaged in devising schemes for the capture of Charles. It was on this occasion that the duke, at their first interview, addressed Sir Alexander in half jocular terms—"Ho! is this the great Rebel of the Isles?" when Sir Alexander tartly replied—"No, my Lord Duke; had I been the Rebel of the Isles, Your Royal Highness would never have crossed the Spey!"

It was so far fortunate, however, that Lady Margaret was at home. She was a lady noted for her great beauty and accomplishments—whose benevolence and charity are still unforgotten in the place—and whose graces and virtues were an honour to the distinguished House of Eglinton, from which she came.

On the arrival of Flora and her attendant at Monkstadt, she requested one of the servants to tell Lady Margaret that she had just called on her way from the Long Island. The heroine was at once shown into the drawing-room, where she found several gentlemen sitting, in military dress, among whom was Captain John Macleod, son of Donald Macleod of Balmeanach, who was in command of a band of militia, then stationed at Uig, about two miles distant. Others of Macleod's men were also in the house at the time.

A lady friend of Flora was also present, Mrs. Macdonald, the wife of John Macdonald of Kirkibost, North Uist, who arrived a few days before from the Long Island, and who had informed Lady Margaret privately, that, in all probability, the prince would soon land in Skye. Among the rest Flora was delighted to meet her good old friend, Mr. Alexander Macdonald of Kingsburgh, *alias* "Alasdair MacDhomhnuill Mhic Alasdair Mhic Ailein," factor for Sir Alexander.

When Flora entered the rather crowded room, the whole company arose to welcome her, as, owing to her long absence in Edinburgh, they had not seen her for years. She was amiable and cheerful, and warmly exchanged the congratulations of her respected friends. Her acute perception, however, led her to suspect that Captain Macleod had an idea in his mind, that her appearance on this occasion was caused by something more important than a mere friendly visit. Under this impression she entered into a free and easy conversation with him, sat beside him, and appeared delighted with his social talk. His conduct towards her was for a time of a very different kind, and indeed scarcely courteous. His language bordered on rudeness, and the questions put by him were positively uncivil.

> Be pleased to tell me, my good lady, whence you came today, whither do you intend to go—by what boat or vessel did you cross the Minch, and who accompanied you?

To all these pointed queries, the gallant maiden, smiling and self-possessed, returned distinct replies in calm and pleasing language; and her deportment was so fascinating and agreeable throughout, that she soon won upon the impertinent officer, at once gained his esteem, and had the honour of being escorted by him to dinner, where she received his most assiduous attention. The questions now asked her were of a less disagreeable character, such as—"What news, Miss Macdonald, from the Long Island? What of that unfortunate rebel, Prince Charles?"

In answer to the latter, Flora smiled and expressed herself in the blandest terms, saying, "Perhaps, Captain Macleod, you are not aware that I am a bit of a Jacobite myself, and I am therefore glad to understand, that the unfortunate fugitive has at last succeeded in effecting his escape from his pursuers, and that, by means of a vessel from France put at his service, he has left the Long Island."

The officer listened attentively, and deemed the truth of the statement highly probable.

At dinner, Lady Margaret sat at the head of the table, and her factor, Kingsburgh, in the absence of her husband, occupied the other end of it. As the guests were numerous, and some of them, such as Flora and Mrs. Macdonald, Kirkibost, exceptionally welcome ones, her Ladyship appeared overjoyed, but expressed regret that her husband was absent, as she seldom had the pleasure of such an interesting company in that remote quarter. All this time, however, her Ladyship was not aware that the prince was in the immediate vicinity of her dwelling.

Flora, always guarded and far-seeing, well knew, that when the secret must soon be revealed to her Ladyship, it would be necessary to send a messenger to the prince and acquaint him of such future proceedings as might be judged advisable to adopt. For this purpose, she had Niel, her own servant, in her eye, as the most suitable medium for the undertaking. In course of the table talk, Captain Macleod, while in the act of dissecting a partridge, asked her Ladyship if there was much ground-game in that quarter; when she replied that they had some snipe and partridges; and that there was great abundance of wild ducks and geese on the adjoining lake of Callum-Cille at all seasons, as well as flocks of wild swans during the month of September. Flora, hearing this, remarked that if there was a fowling-piece about the premises, her servant, Niel, was no ordinary hand at the gun, and he might use it to advantage. Lady Macdonald replied, that there was a great variety of all sorts in the gun-room, where Niel might help himself, and try his luck.

This was what Flora wanted, to afford a pretext for Niel to scamper to the fields, when in reality the safety of the prince was the only game he wished to see after. Shortly after dinner, when the guests betook themselves hither and thither for amusement, Flora managed to get hold of Kingsburgh alone, revealed to him all about the prince, and suggested the necessity of his breaking the intelligence to Lady Margaret, as she could not venture to do it herself, in case she might become so affected by her Ladyship's probable alarm, as to be observed by some of the guests.

Kingsburgh being a cool and sensible gentleman, undertook to perform this important but delicate duty. In about half-an-hour after, he took her Ladyship into a private, apartment, and revealed the whole secret to her. The intelligence, so sudden and unexpected, greatly affected her, so much so indeed, that she all but fell into a fit of hysterics. Her features were convulsed, and she screamed so loudly, as to cause a fear that she might be heard by others in the house. She expressed herself in accents of terror—sat trembling on a chair, and exclaimed— "Oh! dear Kingsburgh, we are undone—we are ruined—we will all have to suffer the penalty of death on the scaffold! O! dear. O! dear, what is this?"

Kingsburgh, with characteristic prudence and serenity of mind, assured her that there was no danger whatever, that he himself would conduct His Royal Highness to Kingsburgh House, and that all would be right in the end.

"Oh," said her Ladyship, "how much I wish that my dear, sterling friend, Captain Donald Roy were here at this moment. I sent him the other day to Fladda-Chuain, as I was told the prince was expected to land there, and he was supplied with shirts and other requisites for his comfort. I hope that he has returned to Shulista, where he is a patient of Dr. Maclean, for the curing of his leg, pierced by a musket ball in the Battle of Culloden. He may now be at home, let him get notice to come immediately."

★★★★★★

Fladda-Chuain is an island in the Minch about a mile long, and distant about eight miles from the shore of Monkstadt. It is not inhabited, but has usually a small hut in it, to afford shelter to fishermen, and to hunters after wild fowl, which frequent it in millions.

Dr. John Maclean who resided at Shulista, about four miles from Monkstadt, was celebrated as a surgeon over all the Western Isles. He was reputed a very learned man, and deeply versed in the Greek and Roman Classics. It has been said of him that he could repeat Homer's *Iliad* and Virgil's Æneid from beginning to end. He possessed an endless store of amusing anecdotes. He had two sons, one of whom was for many years M.P. for a borough in England; and the other Malcolm, a Captain in the British Army, who died, near Shulista, about forty years ago, (as of 1882).

★★★★★★

Donald Roy was accordingly sent for, soon arrived on horseback at Monkstadt, and found Lady Margaret and Kingsburgh walking alone in the garden. By this time, they had less reserve, as Captain Macleod and his men had gone on to Uig to visit their company of military stationed there.

Lady Margaret was greatly cheered by the presence of Donald Roy, though she could not help saying to him—"I fear, my dear Donald, that it is all over with us, and that we are ruined for ever."

"There is not the least fear of that, my Lady, take comfort, as all will succeed well," replied Donald.

By this time Flora made her appearance, with an air of smiling cheerfulness; and her conversation and presence restored her Ladyship to a calm and collected state of mind. They now held a consultation as to the best plan to adopt in the morning; when it was resolved that, in the meantime, the poor prince who had been left for so many hours alone in his cave, must be immediately seen to, and have creature comforts supplied to him. They agreed to send Niel MacEachainn to tell him that Kingsburgh proposed to visit him on the shore very soon. Niel at once performed this duty and speedily returned. In half-an-hour after, he shouldered a musket and scampered across an intervening field, as if in search of game, which, however, was sufficiently safe from Niel's approach, as his musket had neither flint nor ramrod, and he was without powder or shot.

Kingsburgh soon arrived at the cave with some brandy and wine for the prince, as well as something substantial to eat, but no prince was there! Niel who was in advance waited Kingburgh's arrival, and remained in charge of the refreshments, while Kingsburgh set off in search of Charles, and walked across the fields in the direction of the house of Scuddeburgh. At length, on seeing a flock of sheep, moving with all their speed towards the high-grounds, as if scared by some strange object, he beheld in the distance a giant-like figure in female attire, stalking rapidly over the meadow, with every pace a fathom in length, and every movement more fantastic than the most fertile imagination could delineate!

Kingsburgh made up to the ghastly female, who, holding a rough, knotted club in her hand, put the question—"Are you Macdonald of Kingsburgh?"—"I am, your Royal Highness!"—when, after congratulations of no ordinary fervency, the prince said—" Let us now go back to the place I left." This was done, and the much needed refreshments were liberally supplied, and as liberally and thankfully used.

Late in the evening Sir Alexander's cattleman entered the servants' hall at Monkstadt, in a very excited state, and said in his own vernacular—

A Dhe, gleidh sinn! chunnaic mi boirionnach mor a' bras-shiubhal nan raointean, eadar so agus an Dun, le lorg fhada 'na laimh, le currachd neonach air a ceann, agus le eididh iongantach m'a coluinn. Cha n'eil teagamh nach aon i dhiubhsan a ghlais na Sithichean 'nan seomraichibh 'san Dun, agus a fhuair cothrom teichidh. Chan fhaca mi a leithid riamh ann an cruth neach saoghalta.

Lord, preserve us! I saw a large female quickly traversing the fields betwixt this and the fort, with a long stick in her hand, with a curious hood on her head, and with a remarkable dress on her person. Undoubtedly she must be one of those whom the Fairies had locked up in their chambers in the fort, who contrived to escape. I never beheld one to be compared with her in the shape of a worldly creature.

Kingsburgh related this anecdote to the prince, who heartily laughed at it.

Previous to this Niel undeceived the astonished cattleman in the hall, as well as the other menials present, by telling them that the gigantic female in question was no fairy prisoner in Scuddeburgh Fort, but an Irish spinning-maid whom they had ferried from the Long Island, on her way to the residence of Flora Macdonald's mother, at

Armadale.

The prince was now left for the night in a recess on the shore to which Niel had carried blankets and other coverings to afford him comfort.

★★★★★★

It has been stated by some that the prince had removed to some concealed place near the garden at Monkstadt, but this was not the case. He never left the shore and the adjoining fields that evening. It is true that Lady Margaret was very wishful to see His Royal Highness, but could not venture to approach the shore at such an untimely hour in the evening. Besides, Flora advised her Ladyship to keep entirely aloof from the prince, as she (Flora) had all along done to the last moment, as many others may be implicated by combining even privately for effecting his rescue.

★★★★★★

Meanwhile Captain Macleod and his companions returned from Uig to Monkstadt, and had retired for the night. This circumstance afforded the prince's friends a better opportunity for maturing their schemes. Lady Margaret, Flora, and old Kingsburgh, with Captain Donald Roy Macdonald, assembled after midnight in a private room, where they held an earnest consultation as to the means immediately to be adopted. It was arranged that Kingsburgh should take the prince next morning along with him to his own house, twelve miles distant, and then pass him on through Skye to the Island of Raasay. It was further arranged that Donald Roy should that very night make all haste to Portree, the capital of Skye, a distance of twenty miles from Monkstadt, for the purpose of sending for, and of seeing the young laird of Raasay, and securing a suitable boat to ferry the prince to that Island.

Macleod, *alias* "MacGille Challuim," the old laird of Raasay, had embraced, with his clan, the prince's cause; but his son and heir resolved to remain loyal. Father and son adopted this policy with the view of securing their property against forfeiture, in the case of future adverse circumstances coming to pass.

Their arrangements made, the party at Monkstadt retired to enjoy a few hour's rest. Soon after sunrise Kingsburgh, who failed to sleep any during the night, arose and entered the dining-room, where he found Lady Margaret, Flora, and Mrs. Macdonald, Kirkibost, sitting up together at that early hour. Captain Macleod and his party were as yet enjoying their slumbers in another wing of the house, and their absence at that critical hour was neither missed nor regretted. It was believed that the early departure of Kingsburgh that morning would create no suspicion, as he had intimated the previous day at dinner, that he desired to get home, either late that evening or very early on the Sabbath morning.

The old gentleman, accordingly, after an early breakfast and when furnished with suitable refreshments for the journey, joined Betty Burke on the shore, and set off with that sturdy Irish spinster on their rugged way to Kingsburgh House. The morning was calm but misty, and exceedingly wet; the rain fell in torrents. It was deemed prudent to avoid, as much as possible, the ordinary road—which at best in these days, was merely a rough riding-path—and to take the more unfrequented tracks across the moors. This resolution added miles to the length of their journey, yet it was their wish that night would fall before their arrival at Kingsburgh, not knowing what guests might be there before them.

For some time after the departure of Kingsburgh, Flora sat in the breakfast parlour with Lady Margaret, Mrs. Macdonald, Kirkibost; Captain Macleod and others—and when a befitting opportunity offered, she made a motion to take her leave, and to make ready for the journey; whereupon Lady Margaret affected great concern as to her short stay,—deemed it ridiculous that she should think of such a journey in such heavy rain—pressed upon her the propriety of remaining at any rate until next day, and stated that she might be the means of taking Mrs. Macdonald along with her, they having before agreed to go together.

Flora, on the other hand, expressed her great anxiety to get home to Armadale, as speedily as possible, as her dear mother was seriously ill, and, as her ladyship knew, quite alone, in such turbulent times.

After repeated pressings and refusals, Lady Margaret very reluctantly consented to her going, and addressed her—

As you are determined not to remain, dear Flora, I beg that you will wait until the hostler provides suitable ponies, with comfortable saddles, for Mrs. Macdonald and you, to carry you on.

When all was ready, and after shaking hands with Lady Margaret, Captain Macleod, and others, the two ladies mounted their tiny steeds, and trotted away. The faithful Niel MacEachainn, and other two young men who were well acquainted with the hill riding-path, accompanied them on foot. Moving slowly along, the party, after a few hours, overtook Kingsburgh and his Irish maid making the best of their way forward. Ere then, however, the unceasing rain fell in such torrents as to swell the mountain streams to overflowing, and render most of the usual fords almost impassable. Here and there under the shelter of rocks, the party rested to pass the time. Having arrived at a pretty spot, they were directed to a pure spring of water, at which they sat down, and mingled part of its contents with Lady Margaret's mountain-dew.

The well had been pointed out to the drenched party by a boy who was herding cattle at the place, and who, for his activity, received from the big Irish woman the first shilling of which he was ever possessed. His name was John Macdonald, a smart raw-boned lad, bonnetless, and barefooted, who could not talk a vocable of English. He lived to the patriarchal age of one hundred and seven years, and died in Lawn Market of Edinburgh, in 1835, at the house of his son, Donald Macdonald, bagpipe maker to the Highland Society of Scotland.

★★★★★★

A minute account of John Macdonald's life is given in No. 36, of the *Celtic Magazine*, which cannot fail to interest such readers as take pleasure in the incidents connected with the Rebellion of 1745. The writer of these pages is much indebted to good old John for furnishing many particulars connected with the movements of the prince in his pilgrimage through the Isle of Skye.

★★★★★★

Many years after that well was secured by the Kingsburgh family with polished flags, and a chained drinking-cup; and it is called to this day, (1882)—"Tobair a' Phrionnsa," the Prince's Well.

Several ludicrous incidents took place on this rough and uncomfortable journey. Again and again Betty Burke, forgetting her assumed sex, when leaping over streams, and climbing rugged cliffs, managed her ragged skirts with amusing awkwardness. Chambers in his description of this journey informs us that—

In crossing a stream which traversed the road, Charles held up his petticoats indelicately high, to save them from being wet. Kingsburgh pointed out that, by doing so he must excite strange suspicions among those who should happen to see him; and His Royal Highness promised to take better care on

86

the next occasion. Accordingly, in crossing another stream, he permitted his skirts to hang down and float upon the water. Kingsburgh again represented that this mode was as likely as the other to attract attention; and the prince could not help laughing at the difficulty of adjusting this trifling and yet important matter of his dress.

In the afternoon the party were met by numbers of country people returning home from church, who after saluting Kingsburgh, their respected factor, fixed their eyes upon and stared at the uncommon size and slovenly appearance of that Irish lass that strode so reckless-like along! Kingsburgh upbraided them in Gaelic for their unmannerly curiosity, yet, they exclaimed in astonishment—

O! faicibh am boirionnach neonach sin! Faicibh na ceuman mora, fada aig an nighinn ghairbh, ghobhlaich sin! Ochan! nach dana, slaodach, neo-sgiobalta, drabasta an sgliurach i! Is cinnteach gur ann de shliochd 'nam famhar i.

(I see that strange woman! Behold the big, wide steps of that rude, long-legged dame! Eh me! what a bold, untidy, slovenly, uncouth slattern she is! Surely she must be one of the giant race!)

The poor peasants were utterly bewildered, as well they might!

After an uncomfortable day's travelling, the party arrived in safety at the mansion of Kingsburgh, a little before midnight. They had no desire to reach it earlier. The family had all gone to rest. Kingsburgh sent Flora and a servant maid to his wife's bedroom to get her up, in order to prepare a supper for her husband and his guests. The good lady at first declined to leave her couch, thinking that her husband had fallen in with some fugitive rebels in distress, whom he wished to entertain. Flora did not then undeceive her. The good lady sent the keys to her husband, with orders to the company to help themselves to the best cheer they could get at that untimely hour. At that moment her daughter, a little girl, went running up to her mother's bedside, and exclaimed—"Oh! mamma, papa has brought home the most muckle, ill shaken-up wife you have ever cast eyes upon, and brought her into the hall too."

Mrs. Macdonald seeing the necessity for getting up, did so at once, and when about entering the hall, its door half ajar, she observed the gaunt female figure, and at once started back. Kingsburgh, who stood in the passage, desired her to accompany him into the room, which she did with trembling steps, and, on her appearance, the romantic figure quickly advanced, and warmly saluted her. The astonished lady was at once undeceived for she felt the roughness of a male cheek, and the reality that it was no other than the prince himself instantly flashed upon her mind, when she all but fainted. She however speedily retired and in broken accents, addressed her husband—"Oh, dear! O dear, have matters come to this? We are all ruined—we shall all be hanged!"

Kingsburgh, smiling answered—"My dear wife, we shall die but once, and if we die to verify your prediction, we will sacrifice our lives in a good and noble cause. Go now, make haste, and prepare supper for us, we much require it. Get bread, butter, cheese, eggs, or whatever you can lay your hands on, for the poor starving prince will eat anything in the shape of food."

She apologised, and said that she had nothing ready at that untimely hour, but these common things.

"All right," said her husband, "let us have them at once, and come to supper yourself."

"Me come to supper! I know not how to conduct myself before royalty."

"Royalty here, or royalty there, the prince will not sit down without you, and he is as easy and plain as Captain Donald Roy Macdonald, and you know what he is."

While supper was being prepared by Mrs. Macdonald herself, the cook being left in bed, Flora stood beside her, and related all her adventures for the previous two days. The lady remarked that Flora had acted very imprudently in allowing the boat that brought them to Skye to return immediately to the Long Island, as on its arrival, the crew could not escape being seized, and minutely examined; and the consequence would no doubt be, that the royal troops would set out in fresh pursuit.

In this conjecture the good lady proved quite correct—for the boat on its return was instantly captured—the boatmen separately examined, and the sad reality at once expiscated. Captain Ferguson immediately set sail in his government cutter for Skye, and pursued the track of the prince from his landing at Monkstadt, until he finally escaped from the island. This merciless officer was, however, a week too late.

The oversight of allowing the boat to return so soon to Uist, was the only point in which the prudence and judgment of the gallant Flora had ever failed. It is true that she did not suggest or sanction its return, but, unfortunately, she did not give instruction to the contrary; and the crew were no doubt desirous to return to their homes.

Meantime, Mrs. Macdonald of Kingsburgh, assisted by Flora, and Mrs. Macdonald, Kirkibost, prepared supper, at which the prince sat on the right of the hostess, with Flora on her left. After supper, to which the prince did ample justice, the ladies retired, leaving Kingsburgh and his august guest alone. His Royal Highness, apologising for the liberty, produced a small, black, tobacco pipe, which he called "the cutty," and was enjoying a puff from it, while his host prepared hot water, sugar, and mountain dew to make a bowl of toddy.

★★★★★★

In these times, and until a late period, toddy was never made in glass tumblers, but in large punch-bowls, often of Chinese manufacture, and when it was duly mixed the glasses of the guests were filled out of the punch-bowls by silver or wooden ladles. Punch-bowls are still kept in many households, as ornaments or heirlooms from ancestral times.

★★★★★★

He was extremely cheerful, and while enjoying the exhilarating contents of the magic bowl, he assured Kingsburgh that he had never tasted such excellent toddy in his life. He thought that it excelled by far what he had at Borrodale and in the Long Island. He indeed greatly enjoyed himself, after his many fatigues and hardships, and had no desire as yet to retire to bed. Kingsburgh, however, seeing the wisdom and necessity of going to rest, had to perform the disagreeable duty of suggesting the propriety of breaking up the company, but the prince objected. As Chambers so correctly and graphically describes:

After they had emptied the bowl several times, Kingsburgh thought it necessary to hint to the prince that, as he would require to be up and away as soon as possible on the morrow, he had better now go to bed, so that he might enjoy a proper term of sleep. To his surprise, Charles was by no means anxious for rest. On the contrary, he insisted upon another bowl, that they might, as he said, finish their conversation. Kingsburgh violated his feelings as a host so far as to refuse this request, urging that it was absolutely necessary that His Royal Highness should retire, for the reason he had stated. Charles as eagerly pressed the necessity of more drink; and after some good-humoured altercation, when Kingsburgh took away the bowl to put it by,

His Royal Highness rose to detain it, and a struggle ensued, in which the little vessel broke in two pieces, Charles retaining one in his hands, and Kingsburgh holding the other. The strife was thus brought to an end, and the prince no longer objected to go to bed.

★★★★★★

Tradition says that this punch-bowl was of old China, beautifully figured, and would contain about an English quart. It was for centuries an heirloom in the mansions of the Lords of the Isles. Having been broken as stated, in almost equal halves, it was carefully and neatly clasped with silver, and likely it still exists. Chambers states that in 1827, it was in the possession of Colin Macalister of Barr and Cour, who married a daughter of Old Kingsburgh, the little girl of whom mention has been already made.

★★★★★★

He slept soundly until two o'clock in the afternoon, when Kingsburgh entered his bedroom, and told him that it was high time for him to get up, get breakfast, and prepare for the journey to Portree, a distance of about eight miles.

Kingsburgh happened to have a pair of shoes in the house which he had never worn, and these he provided for the accommodation of His Royal Highness. When Charles had shifted the old for the new, Kingsburgh took up the former, tied them together, and hung them up in a corner of the house, observing that they might yet stand him in good stead. Charles asked him what he meant by that, when the old man replied, "Why, when you are fairly settled at St. James, I shall introduce myself by shaking these shoes at you, to put you in mind of your night's entertainment and protection under my roof." Charles smiled at the conceit of the old gentleman, and bade him be as good as his word. Kingsburgh kept the interesting relics, or the greater part of them, to the end of his days.

When the prince was about to be dressed Mrs. Macdonald took her young daughter to act as his hand-maiden, for, as she afterwards told Bishop Forbes, "the deil a preen he could put in." During the process of dressing he could scarcely stand with laughter at the get-up and style of his habiliments; and, after the pinners, gown, hood, and mantle were properly adjusted, he addressed Miss Macdonald, "Oh Miss, you have forgotten my apron. Get me my apron here, for it is a principal part of my dress."

Kingsburgh and his lady afterwards informed their friends that on this occasion he behaved altogether unlike one in danger, but on the contrary as mirthfully as if he had been dressing himself up in women's clothes for a mere frolic.

The ladies who, amid peals of laughter, assisted in dressing Betty Burke in her antique Irish garments, were altogether much amused. They asked for some of the prince's hair, to be preserved as relics, which he smilingly granted by reclining his head upon the end of a sofa, and requesting them to cut off bunches for themselves. While things were thus getting in readiness for the journey the old lady and Flora went to the bedroom just left by the prince, folded up the sheets on which he had slept, and took possession of one each, and there pledged themselves to preserve them folded up and unwashed until their dying-day when these relics would become their winding-sheets. Such was really the case. Flora never parted with this precious memorial. She carried it with her in after life to America, and back to Skye, where it was carefully kept until her mortal remains were wrapped in its folds, and consigned to the grave.

About three in the afternoon of the same day, the thirtieth of June, 1746, the prince warmly embraced the hospitable old lady and her respected husband, and set off on his journey, accompanied only by Flora, and the dutiful Niel Mac-Eachainn. Niel carried with him the substantial Highland dress of a farmer, and a pair of new shoes, all of which Kingsburgh had provided for His Royal Highness. These were to be exchanged for the Irish dress at some convenient distance from the house. When about half-a-mile on their way, Flora walked on, while the prince and Niel entered a hollow between two rocks, where Charles robed himself in his new dress and shoes. Niel, at the same time, carefully preserved and concealed the tattered raiment, and torn "bachules" of Betty Burke, as keepsakes for Kingsburgh of the prince's perilous adventures.

Captain Donald Roy reached Portree on the previous evening and having met young Raasay at the farmhouse of Toutrome, they prepared everything for meeting the distinguished pair from Kingsburgh, and for conveying the prince to the island of Raasay, separated by a channel of a mile or two from Portree.

When the prince and his attendants arrived, they went to the only inn in the village with young Raasay and Donald Roy to procure refreshments. Donald suggested the propriety of the prince's retiring to a place of safety, as there was great danger in remaining longer in a public hostelry, when so many spies and suspicious characters were moving about. He told him that he knew of a cave where he could find shelter until removed under night to Raasay, and that the sooner he resorted to it the better. They all left the inn immediately, except Flora, under a drenching rain.

The time had now come when Charles had to part for ever with his true and faithful protectress, the gallant Flora. With tears in his eyes he laid hold of the heroine's hands, and bade her a tender and affecting farewell. He ardently thanked her for enabling him to escape from the wall of fire by which he had found himself surrounded, and which he never would have got over without her intrepidity and generous aid. He then handed her his portrait in a golden locket, while he tenderly saluted her, and said, in affecting tones, that he yet hoped to meet her at the Court of St. James, where he should be able properly to reward her self-denying heroism—and her ardent devotion and loyalty to her unfortunate prince.

Such were the adventures of three days, and of only three days— but adventures which have immortalised the name of our heroine, and for ever shed a halo of glory over the devotedness of the female heart.

The promises made by His Royal Highness were richly merited, and though he never gained the position to fulfil them, yet his utter forgetfulness of his deliverer's faithful services to him, was to his ad- mirers utterly inexplicable and unpardonable. He lived for upwards of forty-two years after this parting scene on the beach of Portree, and during that long period, he never acknowledged by letter or other- wise the dangers to which Flora exposed herself to save his life.

During the darkness of that night he was conveyed from his cave to Raasay, and thence through Skye to the mainland, where for nearly three months he had to undergo terrible trials and severe hardships. His home was in rocks and in caves, and in mountain recesses, where he passed his weary time hourly exposed and liable to be seized by his vigilant pursuers. At last, fortunately for him, two French vessels, the L'Heureux, and the *Princesse de Conti*, arrived at Lochnanuagh, on one of which he got aboard, and sailed for France on the 20th of Septem- ber, 1746. He died, after having spent a chequered, but, by no means, a too provident career, on the 30th of January, 1788.

The following lines will appropriately close this chapter:—

On the Beach of Portree, Skye, 30th June, 1746.
Amid the shells and shingle on the shore,

The Stuart Prince and Flora met to part;
"Devoted one," he said, "I owe thee more
Than tongue can utter; ever in this heart
My fair preserver's name will hold a place.
I hope, dear Flora, at no distant day,
With mine the throne, and honours of my race,
I can in deeds thy noble deeds repay,
Farewell! thou faithful one!"
                                        Across the sea,
In sunnier lands, where hearts beat not more true,
The Maiden lived not in the memory
Of him whose life to her fond zeal was due.
Forgotten all the goodness and the grace—
Has gratitude for ever taken wing?
Forgotten that kind sympathetic face—
Ingratitude forgetteth everything!

PARTING OF FLORA MACDONALD
AND PRINCE CHARLES

CHAPTER 6

Flora a State Prisoner—From Skye to London and Back

Flora was distinguished for her earnest and faithful devotion to any duty which she considered herself called upon to perform; and on this occasion she performed her noble task amid severe trials and imminent perils. Her prudent measures, patient endurance, and active fortitude never appear to have forsaken her, nor did the hazard of her own life, from the cause which she had espoused, render her for a moment indifferent to the purpose which she had in view, or chill her benevolent exertions in behalf of her fellow sufferers.

Her trials on account of her heroic conduct were such as have seldom fallen to the lot of any female to endure. She was taken to London, where she was kept as a State prisoner for nearly twelve months. An Act of Indemnity was eventually passed, when she was set at liberty, and permitted to return to her native Highland hills. Greater attention could not be paid to any lady, however distinguished, than was paid to her by all classes of the nobility, in the Metropolis and elsewhere; yet her gentle heart longed for the homely welcome which she knew awaited her from her friends in Skye, and in the Long Island. She was, in the words of the bard of Ledaig,—

'G iarraidh dh'ionnsuidh sneachd nan ard-bheann,
'S creagan corrach tir a' cairdeis,
Ged tha cluaintean Shasuinn aillidh;
'S mor gu'm b'fhearr 'bhi measg nan Gaidheal.

'S iomadh buaidh tha, "luaidh, riut sinte,—
Buaidhean nach gabh dhomhsa innseadh;
Buaidhean pearsa, buaidhean inntinn,

94

Buaidhean nach gabh luaidh no sgriobhadh.
Nadur fiachail, fialaidh, finealt',
Ann am pearsa chuimir, dhirich;
Cridhe blath, le gradh air 'lionadh,
'S caoimhneas tlath do dh'ard 's do dh'iosal!

Of which beautiful lines the following is a free version:—

'Mid the pomp of huge London her heart still was yearning
For her home in the corrie, the crag, and the glen;
Though fair be the daughters of England, the fairest
And stateliest walks in the land of the Ben.

What poet may praise her! her virtues to number,
Would baffle the cunning of pencil and pen
Though fair be the casket, the jewel is fairer,—
The best of true hearts, for the best of good men.

She is comely and kind, and of gracefulest greeting,
Erect and well-girt, as a lady should show,
And a heart with warm blood, and a pulse ever beating,
With loving reply to the high and the low!

Before, however, Flora was taken from Skye to London, she had many difficulties to encounter. In a short time, the various movements of the prince through Skye, Raasay, and other adjacent localities soon became known; and the fact of his having been harboured by friendly persons in those quarters soon aroused the energy and zeal of the government officials against all who were known to give him the least aid in effecting his escape. Flora was considered the chief actor in this hazardous adventure. She had, however, a great number of stern coadjutors, and faithful accomplices. Among them were Clanranald and his lady; Donald Roy Macdonald, brother of Hugh Macdonald of Baileshear; Donald Macleod of Galtrigal, Malcolm Macleod, Old Kingsburgh, and several others.

Of all these, none could be more sincere and true to him in his misfortunes than Donald Macleod of Galtrigal. He was a shrewd, ingenious man, and capable of carrying out, with great caution, whatever scheme he might devise for the great object he had in view. Hence, the more eager was the desire of the government officers to capture him, that he might be placed on his trial for his offences. This was accomplished by his own countryman, Major Allan Macdonald of Knock, an officer who had more opportunities than others of ferreting out Donald's movements. Major Allan, commonly called "Ailean a' Chnoic," was a stern, cruel-hearted man, who had but few favourites in his native Isle. He treated the poor Jacobites there with uncalled-for severity, so that he was literally detested by most of his acquaintances, and particularly so by those who had embraced the prince's cause. A certain priest in Uist, who naturally cherished no love for Major Allan, composed some verses to him of the most cutting and satirical description. Of these a few lines may be given:—

Ciod i do bharail air Ailean, a' bheist?
Cha teid e o'n bhaile gu'n iul as a dheigh,
Bithidh chlaidh' air tarsuing, mar gu'n deanadh e tapadh,
B'e sin cuinneag a' mhaistridh, is ceis phaisgte nam breug!

Than dubh-phuill uir Ailean a' Chnoic,
'S ait leam a chluinntinn air Ailean a' Chnoic,
'S gu'm bheil an dubh-phuill air a sparradh gu grinn,
'S gur ait learn a chluinntinn air Ailean a' Chnoic.

Donald Macleod was made prisoner by Major Allan Macdonald, in Benbecula and conveyed to London. He was released in June of the following year, when he was presented by Mr. John Walkinshaw of London, with a handsome silver snuff-box, beautifully chased and gilt. It remained, and likely still remains, a valued heirloom in the posses-sion of his descendants. Donald was one of those well-to-do farmers in Skye, who lived comfortably on their comparatively small tene-ments and paid then from £30 to £60 of rent, a class of respectable farmers now all but extinct.

As soon as it became known for certain that Prince Charles had succeeded in making his way to the mainland, and in ultimately ar-riving in France, the Royal Forces scattered over the Western Isles became much concerned and excited that the object of their research had thus escaped. Greatly annoyed at the failure of their vigilance in guarding the sea-coasts of these rugged Islands, the commanders by sea and land became doubly aroused to the necessity of making the best of an expedition now all but hopeless. They became determined to wreak their vengeance upon the various actors in the stratagem by which the prince had eluded their grasp. Kingsburgh's guilt in this affair was discovered by the captain of one of the government ships. That venerable old gentleman was consequently arrested, sent pris-oner to Fort-Augustus, and thence to Edinburgh Castle, where he was treated with painful severity and cruelty for a whole year.

All his precautions and plans for concealment proved abortive from an incidental circumstance that took place at the time. Two days after the prince had left Kingsburgh, Captain Ferguson of the government war-ship sailed across from the Long Island, the rumour having reached him that the prince had escaped to Skye, and he cast anchor at the Crannag, a harbour close to the Chamberlain's residence. He went ashore for the purpose of procuring fresh provisions and other requisites, when he met a dairymaid attending some cattle in an adjacent field, and entered into conversation with her, as he did indeed with all with whom he came in contact, expecting to elicit something from them relative to the subject of his search.

The unsuspecting maid let fall some expression that arrested the captain's attention as something important or which might lead to it. He asked her if she had ever seen a man-of-war, and in the blandest terms, invited her to go on board the ship, to inspect all that could there be seen. Here the maid was treated with great kindness, and was flattered by receiving several nice presents. Captain Ferguson spoke Gaelic to her, and she thought him the nicest and kindest gentleman she had ever seen. She was asked all the country news, and everything relating to her master,—his name, his occupation, his family,—the name of the place; and such other familiar matters were freely discussed.

The poor girl, ignorant as to who her entertainer was, told him, with an air of unpardonable pride, that she had seen Prince Charles, that he was a night at her master's house, and that his appearance pleased her much, though he did not appear to be half so kind as Captain Ferguson himself was. She stated farther, that the prince's shoes were all torn, that he wore a *cota-clo* (that is a kelt coat) that belonged to Mr. Allan, her master's son. This was all that Ferguson wanted, and in consequence of the girl's imprudent disclosure, the government officials obtained the first direct proof of the prince's motions, and of the manner in which Kingsburgh had acted in securing his escape.

On the same day on which the prince left Kingsburgh House for Portree, the old gentleman, apprehending danger, crossed the hill to the east side of the island, but his pursuers soon discovered him at a place called Lealt. Young Allan, however, managed all along to elude the researches of the government officers and was never captured, though as active as any in the case of the prince. Flora, on the other hand, with her natural gallantry, made no attempts whatever to conceal herself, though she was well aware that she was diligently sought after.

After having parted with the royal fugitive at Portree, she went to spend a few days with her mother at Armadale, and then made the best of her way to her brother's residence at Milton, in the Long Island. She had been only a few days there, when she received a summons to appear for examination before Macleod of Talisker, a Captain of Militia, in the Isle of Skye, to answer all the grave charges made against her. Her friends became alarmed for her ultimate safety, and earnestly importuned her to disregard the summons, and to secret herself for a season amid the mountain fastnesses of her native isle, as her prince had already successfully done. This she peremptorily and indignantly refused to do, saying with her natural magnanimity of soul that as she had done nothing of which she either repented or felt ashamed, she would appear at any tribunal or before any government official, and answer whatever charges might be brought against her.

Unprotected and alone, she set out for Talisker, and Captain Macleod having satisfied himself by committing to writing the various statements which he had elicited from the gentle culprit before him, and with whom he was previously well acquainted, permitted her to visit her mother at Armadale. On her way, she accidentally met with her stepfather returning home from the Long Island, and before evening she was seized by a party of soldiers, who conveyed her a prisoner on board the *Furnace*, commanded by Captain Ferguson.

General Campbell, who happened to be on board, treated the amiable rebel with great kindness and consideration. He allowed her to land at Armadale, under an escort of soldiers, to bid farewell to her mother, to replenish her wardrobe, and to procure a female servant, Kate Macdonald. Meantime her stepfather, the officer of militia who granted passports to Flora, Betty Burke, and the others, to cross from the Long Island to Skye, became afraid that he might be implicated in the plot, and deemed it prudent to retire to a place of concealment.

Had not this officer granted the requisite passports, the gallant Flora could never have conducted the prince from Uist to Skye. These passports were the hinge on which the success of the whole adventure turned.

Flora, now a State prisoner of great importance, was conveyed from Skye on board the *Furnace* to Dunstaffnage Castle, in Argyleshire, where she was confined for about ten days, under the charge of Mr. Niel Campbell, at the time governor of that ancient castle, a place of note in the early history of our country. It was once a royal residence of the kings of Scotland. It is situated on a rocky promontory that juts out into Loch Etive, and is one of the most romantic and secluded places that nature, in all the picturesque beauty of those regions, can present. It is true that the ancient magnificence of the place had passed away long before the gallant Flora became an inmate of its walls, for rescuing from captivity and death, the last of the Stuart race—a prince whose forefathers had long reigned with royal dignity in that sequestrated region.

General Campbell addressed the following note to the governor, introducing his "very pretty young rebel":—

Horse Shoe Bay, 1st August, 1746.

Dear Sir,—I must desire the favour of you to forward my letters by an express to Inveraray; and if any are left with you, let them be sent by the bearer. I shall stay here with Commodore Smith till Sunday morning. If you can't come, I beg to know if you have any men now in garrison at your house, and how many? Make my compliments to your lady, and tell her that I am obliged to desire the favour of her for some days to receive a very pretty young rebel. Her zeal, and the persuasion of those who ought to have given her better advice, have drawn her into a most unhappy scrape, by assisting the young Pretender to make his escape. I need say nothing further till we meet; only assure you that I am, dear Sir, your sincere friend, and humble servant,

John Campbell.

P.S.—I suppose you have heard of Miss Flora Macdonald?—

J.C.

To Neil Campbell, Esq., Captain of Dunstaffnage.

About ten days after, General Campbell addressed another brief note to the same Governor, m the following terms:—

Wednesday Evening,

Sir,—You will deliver to the bearer, John Macleod, Miss Macdonald, to be conducted in his wherry. Having no officer to send, it would be very proper you send one of your garrison alongst with her.— I am, Sir, your most obedient humble servant,

John Campbell.

To the Captain of Dunstaffnage.

During our heroine's short stay at this fortress, the governor's lady,

99

and other friends, paid every possible attention to their fair prisoner. All of them felt much interest in her on account of her accomplished manners and humble deportment. Her society was courted and appreciated by all the respectable families in the neighbourhood, who had been privately invited to meet her as a distinguished State prisoner.

When John Macleod and his wherry arrived to take her away, it was late in the evening; but next morning the preparations for departure were made. After an early breakfast, the governor's lady, with tears in her eyes, handed Flora into the boat. The sails were immediately set, and before a stiff breeze, the frail craft glided swiftly down Loch Etive, towards the Sound of Mull, and soon disappeared.

It is probable that John Macleod and the Dunstaffnage officer conveyed Miss Flora to Glasgow, as some days afterwards our fair captive was put on board the *Bridgewater*, commanded by Commodore Smith, in Leith Roads. During the detention of the *Bridgewater*, at this port, for nearly three months, the fame of our heroine had spread far and near, and she became the object of much public interest. On board Flora met Captain O'Neal, and several others of her countrymen who had, like herself, been arrested, and for the same cause. The commander and all the inferior officers vied with each other in offering civility to their interesting prisoner. Though she was not permitted to leave the vessel, persons of every rank, clerical and lay, and of all shades of politics, were freely allowed to go on board to visit her.

Day after day hundreds of the aristocracy of the metropolis flocked to see the spirited young lady, and many valuable gifts were made to her, as tokens of their esteem. Among those visitors, the clergymen of Edinburgh and Leith of almost every denomination paid their respects to her. Bishop Forbes was very attentive—as also Lady Mary Cochrane, Lady Bruce, and Lady Clark. The latter, in her enthusiasm to honour the modest Highland maid, who enabled Prince Charles Edward to elude his foes, was "willing to wipe her shoes." Lady Cochrane asked as a special favour to be permitted to stay all night on board, and the request was granted; her Ladyship stating that she made the request that she might be enabled afterwards to say that she had passed a night with Flora Macdonald.

The quiet demeanour of the heroine during the vessel's stay at Leith was admired by all who had seen her. The Episcopal clergyman of the place described her, and the scenes on board, in these terms:—

Some that went on board to pay their respects to her used to take a dance in the cabin, and to press her much to share with them in the diversion, but with all their importunity, they could not prevail with her to take a trip. She told them at present her dancing days were done, and she would not readily entertain a thought of that diversion till she should be assured of her prince's safety, and perhaps not till she should be blessed with the happiness of seeing him again. Although she was easy and cheerful, yet she had a certain mixture of gravity in all her behaviour, which became her situation exceedingly well, and set her off to great advantage. She is of a low stature, of a fair complexion, and well enough shaped. One would not discern by her conversation that she had spent all her former days in the Highlands, for she talks English easily, and not at all through the Erse tone. She has a sweet voice, and sings well; and no lady, Edinburgh-bred, can acquit herself better at the tea-table, than what she did when in Leith Roads. Her wise conduct in one of the most perplexing scenes that can happen in life,— her fortitude and good sense—are memorable instances of the strength of a female mind, even in those years that are tender and inexperienced.

On the 7th of November, 1746, the *Bridgewater* weighed anchor amid the display of flags and the cheers of thousands, to carry the fair prisoner and others to London, to stand their trial on a charge of treason. On reaching the great Metropolis, the government discovered that so deeply was the sympathy of the nation excited in Flora's behalf that it would not be prudent to commit her to a common prison, and that it would not by any means conduce to their popularity to visit a young lady with the stern inflictions of the law,—and more particularly so, as her guilt consisted only in one of the most generous actions of humanity; an action too, the performance of which exposed her own life to the most imminent clanger. After a short confinement in the Tower, with many others from the Western Isles, who had been engaged in the same cause, she was handed over to the custody of friends who became responsible to the government for her appearance when demanded. In this mitigated imprisonment Flora remained a State prisoner for nearly twelve months, until, in 1747, the Act of Indemnity, already alluded to, was passed, and she was set at liberty.

During her long imprisonment, if it may be so called, she maintained a cheerful temper, an easy, elegant, and winning address, and appeared most agreeable to all her visitors. A subdued and modest gravity on her part, deepened the interest excited by her simple artless character. Immediately after she received her freedom, she became the guest of Lady Primrose of Dunnipace, where she was visited, and loaded with honours, by distinguished persons of all ranks and classes of the nobility. All admired the dauntless part she had acted, and her case excited so much interest, that she had the honour of a visit from Frederick, Prince of Wales, father of King George the Third. His Royal Highness asked her how she dared to assist a rebel against his father's throne? when she replied, with great simplicity but firmness, that she would have done the same thing for him had she found him in like distress. The prince was so struck with this reply and her artless manner, that he afterwards interested himself to procure for her every comfort.

Meanwhile, the street in which Lady Primrose lived was, day after day, thronged with the carriages of such as desired to see the fair deliverer of Prince Charles. Artists waited upon her to procure her portrait, others to award their gifts; and altogether Flora could never understand how such a simple act of humanity should produce so much excitement, or confer upon her, what she considered, such unmerited celebrity.

When her liberation was announced, and when made aware that she was freely privileged to return to her native Highlands, she respectfully solicited as a special favour, that her fellow-prisoners from the Western Isles should receive the same liberty as herself. She particularly interested herself in behalf of Old Kingsburgh, a State prisoner in Edinburgh, for sheltering the prince in his house. This hospitable gentleman acted all along, as he thought himself, in a very cautious manner, in reference to the royal fugitive. He was not personally much inclined to interfere in the dangerous enterprise, but being at the time Sir Alexander Macdonald's Chamberlain, Lady Margaret, who had a warm feeling for the prince, brought her influence to bear upon him, and did all in her power to induce him to do his best under the trying emergency.

Flora, however, succeeded in procuring his freedom, as also that of Donald Macleod of Galtrigal, Calum Mac Iain Mhic Iain, who went in the capacity of guide to the prince from the Island of Rasaay to Kilmorie, in Strathaird, and also of Niel Macdonald, her servant, commonly called Nial Mac Eachainn Mhic Sheumais (Neil the son of Hector, the son of James), who subsequently followed the prince to France, and, as already stated, became the father of Field-Marshal Macdonald, Duke of Tarentum, one of Napoleon's ablest generals. All these, and others, were liberated through Flora's solicitations at headquarters. When matters were fully and finally arranged, our heroine, with her faithful Nial Mac Eachainn, left London in a coach and four for the Scottish Metropolis.

During this journey of several days, the exuberance of Niel's spirits could hardly be restrained within proper bounds. He was naturally an active, lively, and manly youth, possessed of considerable wit, and no small share of poetic genius. He, as well as most of his companions, never expected to return. On the contrary, they were fully prepared to fall victims on account of their offences against the laws of their country. It is related that Old Kingsburgh, despairing of ever again seeing his family and home, made a hasty will of all his effects before he left Skye. The gallant Flora herself was the most hopeful that no injury would befal her, and that her personal safety stood in no danger. She reasoned in this way: that she had done nothing wrong, and that all her actions in that great tragedy of her life were based, not on political principles, but on the Scriptural laws of humanity and kindness.

Niel MacEachainn composed the following after his liberation:—

Thugadh, Ochan! air falbh mi blio Eilean mo ghraidh.
Gu dol suas dh'ionnsuidh Lunnain gu"m chrochadh gu'n dail;
Air son gu'n d'thug mi furtachd do Thearlach an aigh,
Gus am faigheadh e ann an tearuinteachd 'null thar sail!

Bha Fionghal Nighean Roanuill a' daonan rim' thaobli,
Chum mo stiuireadh le gliocas, 's le misnich ro threin;
Bha i deas agus dileas a dhionadh an laoich,
Bha gun charaid co dian rit.li' 'n ait' eile fo'n ghrein!

A nis fhuair sinn ar saorsa o dhaorsa na truaigh,
Chum gu'm pill sinn air 'n ais dh'ionnsuidh Eilein ar breith;
'S thugadh cliu do'n Oigh mhaisich nach comas a luaidh,
Leis an fhilidh a's ealant' gu seinn as a leth!

Chaidh sinn cuideachd air falbh, 's thain sinn cuideachd air ais,
Ann an carbad ceithir-chuidh'leach 's da chaigeann each,
Is tha aoibhneas, a's gleadhraich, 's ceol-fhuaim nach' eil tais,
'A toirt suaimhneis is spionnaidh do'n chridhe aig gach neach!

Thug am Prionnsa an Fhraing air, ach chithear e ris,
Dhruideadh mach as an tir e, ach leanar a cheum;
'S biodh Nial Mac Eachainn Mhic Sheumais a ris fo chis,

Mar grad-ghreas e gu Tearlach, 'na ruith is 'na leum.

Ochan! Fhionghail Nighinn Raonuill, gum b' eutrom do cheum,
'Dol a dh'fhaicinn do Thearlaich air ardach' mar righ,
'Sa chur failt air 'da luchairt, le 'chrun-oir nan seud,
Is e 'riaghladh na rioghachd, le ciuineas 's le sith!

On the arrival of the party in Edinburgh, Flora remained with kind friends for about three weeks, retaining her faithful valet, Niel Mac Eachainn, and the Skye girl, Kate Macdonald, as her trusty bodyguards. During her stay in the Scottish Metropolis, where she had been for three years previously prosecuting her education, she lived very much in privacy. She had been wearied with the amount of attention previously paid to her. From Edinburgh she made the best of her way to Inverness, where she had some respected friends, who made her their guest for about ten days.

At that period the public roads betwixt Inverness and Skye had not been formed, and the only access to that Island was by rough riding-paths over the intervening hills and dales. Hugh Macdonald, her stepfather at Armadale, in Skye, sent a horse and saddle all the way to Inverness, to convey her to her mother's house, where she arrived in safety, and was affectionately received by her fond mother. She complained of nothing particularly except her fingers, which were blistered and bleeding from holding the bridle, on such a rough and lengthened journey.

★★★★★★

Hugh Macdonald was one of the most powerful men of his clan. He was blind of an eye, which he lost by the branch of a tree, when a mere youth; hence he was called Uisdean Cam Mac Shoirle Mhic Sheumais Mhoir Mhic Dhomhnuill Ghuirm Oig, and was the seventh in lineal descent from Domhnull Gorm Mar, who lost his life by a barbed arrow that pierced his thigh, aimed from the battlement of Eileandonnan Castle in Kintail. Hugh hardly ever met with his equal in wrestling, and other feats of strength.

★★★★★★

CHAPTER 7

Flora's Return to Skye

Having satisfied her mother with full and particular details of all her adventures and perils, she took leave of her for a time, that she might once more have the pleasure of visiting Lady Clanranald at Ormiclade, and her brother at Milton, in Uist. Nearly two months had, however, elapsed before she accomplished this journey, in consequence of detentions by the way. She visited her friends at Scalpa, Raasay, Scorribreck, Kingsburgh, Flodigarry, and specially at Monkstadt, where Lady Margaret and Sir Alexander Macdonald rejoiced at her appearance. On her arrival at Scorribreck, near Portree, where she parted with the prince, Mr. Nicolson, tenant of Scorribreck, and his lady, welcomed her with marked enthusiasm.

After a stay there of a few days, Mr. Nicolson invited a large party of the neighbouring ladies and gentlemen to the hospitable house of Scorribreck to meet the distinguished stranger. Among the rest was Major Allan Macdonald (Ailean à Chnoic), who had, by a cunning device, arrested Flora's friend, Donald Macleod of Galtrigal, and was the cause of his imprisonment. When the major entered the drawing-room, and received the ordinary congratulations of the company, he held out his hand to Flora, whereupon she tartly expressed herself.—

Yes, Sir, I give you my hand, but not entirely with my heart. I wish to show all courtesy to the profession which you have disgraced by a low and base stratagem, utterly unworthy of the conduct of a soldier, a Highlander, and a gentleman!

This piquant repartee, for a moment, paralysed the whole company.

Having made a few other visits to respectable families in the neighbourhood of Portree, where all were delighted to see her, Flora resorted to the mansion-house of Kingsburgh, the residence of her future father-in-law, Mr. Alexander Macdonald, but found on her arrival that the old gentleman, who had but lately returned from his imprisonment in Edinburgh Castle, had gone to Flodigarry, in the north end of the island, where his son, Allan, resided.

★★★★★★

It may appear strange to many that the mansion-house of Kingsburgh, where the prince, Dr. Johnson, Boswell, and many others, shared its hospitality, was merely a heath-thatched cottage, surrounded by a few trees. At that period, it is said, that there were only three slated houses in the island, except Armadale and Dunvegan Castles, and one of the three was a prison. The thatched houses, however, were warm, comfortable, and well furnished.

★★★★★★

Flodigarry, which is a beautiful and romantic place, and is about sixteen miles distant from Kingsburgh, was rented at the time by Allan. The scenery around it is exceedingly grand. The low grounds are studded with small natural tumuli, grass-covered and green, probably the result of ancient glaciers or convulsions of nature. Above it is the serrated towering cliffs of the far-famed Quiraing, frowning in their stern majesty. To the east, the broad Sound of Gairloch, with Loch Staffin and its little Isle, lie fully in view; while on the opposite coast, the Gairloch hills, in successive vistas, and the projecting Seann-Rudha, are seen stretching away in soft and distant perspective.

Close at hand, the Bay of Steinscholl presents itself, with its rough boulder-strewn shore to resist the fury of the Atlantic waves, while a little farther on the eye rests upon the basaltic walls of Garafad, shivered into ghastly shapes, and cloven into huge gorges and fissures, which resound by the thundering roll of the dashing waves. In short, Flodigarry, the home of our heroine for many years, is a spot of rare beauty.

Flora after a short stay at this romantic place, impatient to see Lady Margaret, set off on horseback, and in little more than an hour, arrived at the residence of her chief, at Monkstadt. She was warmly embraced by her Ladyship, with whom she had always been a great favourite. A few days after her arrival at Monkstadt she was taken suddenly and seriously ill. Lady Margaret became painfully alarmed, and despatched an express for Sir Alexander, at the time on a visit at Dunvegan Castle. Without a moment's delay, the only medical man in the island was sent for, and the first illness under which the devoted Flora had ever been known to suffer, caused much anxiety in the whole family.

Fortunately, however, before either Sir Alexander or the medical attendant arrived, the invalid took a favourable turn, and recovered almost as speedily as she had been taken ill. During her stay at Monkstadt, which lasted more than three weeks, the house was frequented by a great many visitors and guests. Sir Alexander, in honour of his fair namesake, got up a splendid banquet, to which all the principal families in the island were invited, together with a number of the Government officers still sojourning in Skye. The festivities extended over four days, when high and low were entertained in a manner that did credit to the friendly generosity and hospitality of the great MacDhomhnuill of the Isles. Among the party were Flora's brother from Milton, Clanranald, and his lady.

It was on this occasion that the arrangements were made, chiefly by Lady Margaret, for Flora's marriage with Allan Macdonald, Kingsburgh's son. For some years before, when Flora and her intended were in their teens, it was well known to their friends that an attachment existed between them. Lady Margaret, at a friendly party in the house one evening, jocularly conversed about this alliance, saying, in her well-known frank and affable manner, that about-to-be married people were always subjects for speculation, and that on this occasion she was to speculate a little herself.

One thing, she said, was apparent, that Allan and Flora resembled one another in tempers, characters, and ages—and they even resembled each other in person—and that they were no doubt intended for one another. Flora modestly replied, that the step her Ladyship alluded to was the most important in a woman's life; but that in regard to the proposals made, while she had no objections to them, as Mr. Allan possessed the esteem of all who knew him, yet, for various reasons, she could not think of such an event taking place for two or three years to come.

The fact was that Flora's judgment was of a practical kind, and her prudence possessed a masculine strength while tempered with feminine delicacy. She knew well that the nature of old Kingsburgh's duties as a public functionary, however honourable, caused him considerable embarrassment, owing to his absence in Edinburgh Castle for a whole year, and that Allan's affairs would naturally be similarly affected. She had, therefore, a presentiment that troubles and anxieties might henceforth fall to her lot, and that it would be prudent to

107

delay their intended union for some indefinite period. Her ideas were known to be only too well founded, and in consequence the matter was no longer pressed. Shortly after this, Flora bade farewell to Lady Margaret and Sir Alexander, and took passage with her brother in a wherry to his residence in the Long Island.

There is nothing remarkable in the history of our heroine for upwards of two years after this. During that period, she spent her time in frequent visits to Lady Clanranald at Ormiclade, and other respectable families in the Long Island. On several occasions she crossed to the Isle of Skye, to wait upon her friends at Monkstadt, and particularly to pass months on end with her mother at Armadale.

★★★★★★

About this time she appears, from the following letter, to have again visited London. The letter is from her old servant, Niel MacEachainn, who, it will be seen, signs himself Macdonald:—

Paris, February 28th, 1749. Dear Florry,—I've often had it in my head to write you since I parted with you at Edinburgh, but as I did not know how long you stayed there, I was at a loss for a direction, but as yr. wellfare is always agreeable to me, it gives me pleasure to hear the reason that has brought you back to London. I hope you will make it your endeavour to deserve as much as in you lyes, the protection of those worthy people that has took you by the hand. I am perfectly acquainted with some of their characters, though I have not the honour to be known to them.

The gentleman who delivers this is a friend of mine, and I hope that is enough to make you exert yourself, among the honest and worthy, to help him to dispose of some valuable toys he has upon hand. I am sure it must give you a sensible joy to hear the person you once had the honour to conduct, is in perfect good health. Soon may they enjoy any other blessings the world can give. Clanranald has his kindest compliments to you, and hopes next time you meet, you'll both be in better spirits than when he last saw you. He and I dined with somebody the very day they were took. Good God, what a fright we got! Give yr. letters to this gentleman, and believe me, Dear Florry, yr. affect friend, and humble servant.

(Signed)   N. Macdonald.

★★★★★★

At length the time appointed for her marriage arrived, and this event, so important to her, took place at Flodigarry, on the 6th of November, 1750. It is almost superfluous to say that the wedding festivities were conducted on a large scale, and lasted for the greater part of a week. The company was unusually numerous, and consisted of almost all the gentlemen in Skye and the Long Island, many of them with their ladies. The bride, robed in a dress of Stuart tartan, with which she was presented when in London by a lady friend, on condition that she would wear it at her marriage, looked remarkably well. All present admired her calm, modest demeanour, appropriately described by the bard:—

A Fhionnaghail chaoimh chaoimhneil,
'S iu sgathan gach maighdinn,
'S an reul iuil tha 'toirt soillse
Dhoibh dh' oidhche 's do lo,
'S oigh uasal air chinnte,
An ribhinn ghlan og;
De Chlann Domhnuill do rireadh,
An ribhinn ghlan og;
'S gur ailleagan ciatach
An ribhinn ghlan og.

The means adopted to furnish accommodation for such a vast assemblage was both amusing and romantic. An immense barn was fitted up for gentlemen's sleeping berths, and a similar place for ladies, while a temporary pavilion was reared, and roofed with heather, to serve alike as a banqueting-hall and a ballroom.

It may be remarked, that the expenses connected with displays of this description, would be naturally looked upon as ruinous to those immediately interested; but nothing of the kind. The customs of the country in those days prevented any thing of this sort. On occasions of such festivities, even when the parties interested in them were well-to-do, the practice was that the guests privately contributed, as each thought proper, to the cellars and larders of the parties about to be married. In this way all creature comforts of every description, solid and liquid, were furnished on a scale of abundance which was indeed extravagant, and more than sufficient to serve the company, should it be requisite, three times over!

After this happy union, Mr. and Mrs. Macdonald spent several years in domestic felicity at Flodigarry, where some of their children were born. Old Kingsburgh by this time had become aged and frail, and having eventually gone the way of all living, was succeeded at Kingsburgh by his son, Allan, who removed from Flodigarry. Flora thus became the lady of the mansion wherein the prince was sheltered through her instrumentality for a night several years before. Kingsburgh was not an estate or property, as many suppose, but a large farm given first to his factor and afterwards to the factor's son by the proprietor, Sir Alexander Macdonald, at a nominal rent.

Allan Macdonald is said to have been one of the most handsome and powerful Highlanders of his clan, and possessed of all the qualities of body and mind which constitute the real gentleman. Boswell, whom he entertained with Dr. Johnson, describes him as:

> One who was completely the figure of a gallant Highlander, exhibiting the graceful mien and manly looks which our popular Scotch song has justly attributed to that character. He had his tartan plaid thrown around him, a large blue bonnet with a knot of black ribbon like a cockade, a brown short coat, a tartan waistcoat with gold buttons, a bluish philibeg, and tartan hose. He had jet-black hair, tied behind, and was a large stately man, with a steady sensible countenance.

Such was the man to whom the gallant Flora yielded her hand and her heart in the thirtieth year of her age. Having removed to Kingsburgh, where she spent a considerable part of her matrimonial life, she often reflected on the fact that her place of abode was the domicile where she had found a night's rest for the unfortunate fugitive for whom she suffered so much, and also the house where she and her husband hospitably entertained Dr. Johnson, and his friend Boswell, while on their Highland tour in 1773, a tour of which Courtney says:—

> *We see the Rambler, with fastidious smile,*
> *Mark the lone tree, and note the heath-clad Isle;*
> *But when the heroic tale of Flora charms,*
> *Decked in a kilt, he wields a cheftain's arms;*
> *The tuneful piper sounds a martial strain,*
> *And Samuel sings, The King shall have his ain!*

The great moralist was evidently much gratified with his reception at this hospitable mansion. He asked Flora as a special favour to be

Flora Macdonald meeting Doctor Johnson

allowed to sleep in the bed which was occupied by the unfortunate prince, and his request was cheerfully granted. Not only so, but Flora added, to the great gratification of her learned guest, that she would furnish him with the identical sheets on which the prince had lain. Dr. Johnson who was not at all times easily pleased, was greatly delighted with the kind attention and unobtrusive demeanour of his distinguished hostess, whom he describes as "A woman of middle stature, soft features, gentle manners, and elegant presence." This was indeed a great compliment from one who was never known to flatter. In a letter to his friend, Mrs. Thrale, he wrote:—

Flora told me, she thought herself honoured by my visit; and I am sure, whatever regard she bestowed upon me, was liberally repaid. If thou likest her opinion, thou wilt praise her virtues.

In the morning on which he left Kingsburgh, a slip of paper was found on his toilet table, with these Latin words written in pencil:— *Quantum cedat virtutibus aurum*, which Boswell translated in these terms:—"*With virtue weighed, what worthless trash is gold!*" undoubtedly high praise from the pen of the learned but prejudiced moralist!

★★★★★★

Vide Boswell's Journal of a Tour to the Hebrides, in which many minute particulars are given relative to the prince and his friends at Kingsburgh, as well as Johnson's visit to that quarter. That *Journal* is rendered doubly interesting, by a great variety of learned and valuable notes appended to it, by the powerful, graphic pen of our late worthy and learned townsman, Dr. Carruthers.

★★★★★★

At the time of this visit of Johnson and his friend to the Hebrides, it could no longer be concealed that Kingsburgh, in the face of all his endeavours to the contrary, had become greatly embarrassed in his pecuniary matters. This arose from no mismanagement or extravagance on his part, or on that of his prudent wife, but from heavy losses which his father, Kingsburgh, sustained in means and property, in consequence of the part he took in the prince's cause, and to his removal from the personal management of his affairs by a year's seclusion in Edinburgh. The old gentleman's losses and liabilities were very great, and he was much disheartened; and, to add to his misfortunes, he was deprived of the remunerative management, as factor, of his chief's extensive estates. In these distressing matters, Allan became naturally entangled, as his father's representative.

CHAPTER 8

Flora and Her Husband Emigrate to North Carolina

At that period, many respectable families from Skye emigrated to America, owing to a general depression in the price of cattle, and other untoward circumstances. Allan determined to follow his countrymen across the Atlantic, with his wife and family, in the hope of repairing his fortune, and of rendering himself independent. The embarrassments of her husband only tended to show the true nobleness of Flora's character. She who had risked her life with her prince was ready and willing to sacrifice everything for a husband's comfort, and to accompany him to whatever quarter of the world it might be expected that fortune might yet smile on the ruined family, Consequently, in the month of August, 1774, Kingsburgh and family sailed in the ship *Baliol*, from Campbelton, Kintyre, to North Carolina.

They had a very favourable passage to the Western World. The time of their departure from Scotland became known among their countrymen in Carolina, where they were anxiously expected and joyfully received on their arrival. Flora's fame preceded her for years; and her countrymen of whom there were hundreds in the colony, felt proud of the prospect of having her presence among them. Various demonstrations, on a large scale, were made to welcome her to American territory. Soon after her landing, a largely attended ball was given in her honour at Wilmington, where she was gratified by the great attention paid to her daughter Anne, then entering into womanhood, a young lady of surpassing beauty.

An American gentleman, speaking of Flora's reception on this occasion, says, that:

113

On her arrival at Cross-Creek she received a truly Highland welcome from her old neighbours and kinsfolk, who had crossed the Atlantic years before her. The strains of the piobaireachd, and the martial airs of her native land, greeted her on her approach to the capital of the Scottish Settlement. In that village she remained for some time visiting and receiving visits from friends, while her husband went to the western part of Cumberland in quest of land.

Many families of distinction pressed upon her to make their dwellings her home, but she respectfully declined, naturally preferring a settled place of her own. She spent about half-a-year at Cameron's Hill, in Cumberland, where she and her family were regular worshippers in a Presbyterian Church at Long Street, under the pastoral care of a countryman, the Rev. Mr. Macleod.

In 1775, her daughter, Anne, became the wife of Major Alexander Macleod of Glendale, Moor County, a gallant youth and a Skyeman, who subsequently distinguished himself in the European wars, and rose to the rank of Major-General in the British service.

★★★★★★

The author was furnished, to a great extent, with the facts here given, from the lips of Flora's daughter, the said Mrs. Major-General Macleod, as well as from the diction of old men in Skye. James Banks, Esq., Fayetteville, N.C., also contributed largely to the account of Flora's American adventures.

★★★★★★

Mrs. Major-General Macleod (that is, Flora's daughter Anne) died in the house of her daughter, Mary, at the village of Stein, in Skye, in 1834. She was a highly accomplished, most agreeable old lady, and she delighted to give minute details of the adventures of her distinguished mother. Her eldest son, an officer in the army, happened to be at Fort-George on the occasion of a Northern Meeting Ball at Inverness, which he attended, when a dispute arose between himself and Glengarry, which resulted in a duel, in which poor Macleod was killed.

Unfortunately for Flora and her family, on their arrival in the New World the American war was about its commencement, and young Kingsburgh soon became involved in its troubles. In 1775, Governor Martin determined to raise among the Scotch Highlanders a body of men to be sent to Boston, and mustered them into the Royal Highland Emigrant Regiment, the better to enable General Gage to look down all opposition in that quarter. Seeing the distinction and honour which all classes of Highlanders awarded to Flora and her husband Kingsburgh, the crafty governor resolved to invest him with the chief command, and, accordingly, granted him the commission of Brigadier-General, an honour which proved a deep source of grief to Flora. An American writer says:

In order to assemble the Scotch, balls were given in different parts of the settlement, some of which Flora attended, with her daughter, Mrs. Major Macleod, and her younger daughter Fanny. Upon these occasions, Anne and Fanny reigned supreme, and bore off the honours of the ballroom.

Early in January, 1776, Allan Macdonald purchased a tract of land from Caleb Touchstone, on the borders of Richmond and Montgomery Counties, and named the place Killiegray. While residing here, a severe typhus fever attacked the younger members of the family, and two of Flora's children died, a boy and a girl, aged respectively 11 and 13. To add to the mother's grief, her husband was absent at his official duties, and was not permitted even to attend the funeral of his beloved children. The present owner of Killiegray, (1882), has fenced in the graves of these children, to preserve the spot sacred to the memory of Flora's offspring.

When the royal banner was unfurled at Cross Creek in 1776, and the loyalist army marched towards Brunswick, under the command of General Donald Macdonald, Allan of Kingsburgh had his own duties allotted to him as Brigadier-General. Flora, with the due devotion of an affectionate wife, followed her husband for many days, and encamped one night with him in a dangerous place, on the brow of Haymount, near the Arsenal of the United States. For a time, she would not listen to her husband's earnest entreaties that she should return home, as his own life was enough to be in jeopardy. Next morning, however, when the army took up its line of march, midst banners streaming in the breeze, and martial music floating on the air, Flora deemed it high time to retrace her steps. She affectionately embraced her husband, and her eyes were dimmed with tears as she breathed to heaven a fervent prayer for his safe and speedy return to his family and home. But alas! she never saw him again in America.

Who can conceive the many anxious days and sleepless nights that the spirited heroine passed in these turbulent and bloody times? afraid that every messenger who arrived was a messenger to announce the death of her gallant husband. She still continued calm, peaceful, and resigned in her demeanour, yet her heart was sad. The revolutions around her were so rapid, the plots and intrigues of the enemy so various, that she could not resist the fear of danger to him on whom her existence and her happiness, in a strange land, depended. Each passing day placed her in a position where her mind hovered between hope and fear; but her prayers and aspirations were silently directed to that Merciful Being, in whose hands are the issues of peace and war, and in Him alone she placed her confidence and trust!

The defeat of the loyalist army, and the capture of her husband at Moore's Creek, struck a knell of woe to her heart. The officers were arrested and imprisoned, and Kingsburgh was committed to the prison of Halifax, Virginia. She had now but few of her family to comfort her. Her five sons were absent, engaged in the service of their country. Her daughter Anne, Major Macleod's wife, was settled in a house of her own, and her daughter Fanny, still in precarious health, from the dregs of the recent fever, was too young to sympathise with a mother in deep distress. Such an accumulation of harrowing visitations could not but press severely even upon the mind of this superior woman.

After many difficulties with the scouts of the enemy, she resolved, on the recommendation of her imprisoned husband, to return, if possible, to her native country. She happened, at a social party, to secure the favour and good offices of Captain Ingram, an American officer, who promised to do his best to forward her views. Some little time after he was able to furnish her with a passport to Fayetteville and Wilmington. Thence she found her way to Charleston, from which port she sailed to her native land, in 1779, leaving her husband still a prisoner in Halifax jail. This step she took at the earnest entreaties of her husband (whom she was not permitted to visit), for the benefit of the health of her daughter Fanny.

Crossing the Atlantic, with none of her family but Fanny (for her five sons and son-in-law were actively engaged in the prevailing war), the gallant Flora met with the last of her adventures. The vessel in which she sailed was met by a French privateer, and a smart action took place. During the engagement Flora refused to take shelter below, but prominently appeared on deck, where, with her wonted magnanimity, she inspired the sailors with courage, and assured them of success. Unfortunately, her left arm was broken in the conflict, and she was afterwards accustomed to say that she had fought both for the House of Stuart and for the House of Hanover, but had been worsted in the service of each.

Flora had seven children—five sons and two daughters—besides three who died young. All her sons were officers who distinguished themselves in the service of their king and country. Charles, the eldest, was a captain in the Queen's Rangers, and was a very accomplished man. Alexander, the second, was a captain of marines, and of high professional character. James, the fourth, served in the Tarlton British Legion, and was a brave officer. John, the fifth surviving son, was a lieutenant-colonel, and had a numerous family. Her daughters, on the other hand, became the wives of officers. Anne as has been said, was the wife of Major General Alex. Macleod. Her second daughter, Fanny, married Lieutenant Donald Macdonald, of Cuiderach, in Skye. (See Appendix for an account of Flora Macdonald's descendants).

After Flora's return from America to her native country, having been absent for about five years, she kept up a considerable correspondence with friends in different quarters of the kingdom. Two of her letters written in 1780 and 1782, are preserved in the Jacobite Memoirs. These were penned while her husband was still in Halifax prison, and her sons still engaged in the service of their country. She was then about sixty years of age. The letters are valuable, as they show that she was an accomplished woman, an affectionate mother, and a devoted wife. They show further, that the source of her cheerful temper and serenity of mind was a steadfast, well-grounded faith in the goodness and mercy of that great Being whom she served, and was willing to trust in all the affairs of life.

The two letters preserved, were addressed to the lady of the late Sir Alexander Muir Mackenzie, of Delvin, near Dunkeld, who paid great attention to Flora's son, Alexander, who, when a boy, lived for nearly three years with this kind family at Delvin, where he was treated as if he had been one of their own children.

The first is in the following terms:—

Dunvegan, Skye, 12th July, 1780.
Dear Madam,—I arrived at Inverness the third day after parting with you, in good health, and without any accidents, which I always dread. My young squire continued always very obliging and attentive to me. I staid at Inverness for three days. I had the good luck to meet with a female companion from that to Skye. I was the fourth day, with great difficulty, at Raasay, for my hands being so pained with the riding.

117

I have arrived here a few days ago with my young daughter, who promises to be a stout Highland "Caileag," quite overgrown of her age. Nanny and her family are well. Her husband was not sailed the last account she had from him.

I have the pleasure to inform you, upon my arrival here, that I had two letters from my husband, the latter dated 10th May. He was then in very good health, and informs me that my son Charles has got the command of a troop of horse in Lord Cathcart's regiment; but alas! I have heard nothing since I left you about my son Sandy, which, you may be sure, gives me great uneasiness. But I still hope for the best.

By public and private news, I hope we will soon have peace reestablished, to our great satisfaction, which, as it's a thing long expected and wished for, will be for the utility of the whole nation—especially to poor me, that has my all engaged. Fond to hear news, and yet afraid to get it.

I wait here till a favourable opportunity for the Long Island shall offer itself. As I am upon all occasions under the greatest obligations to you, should you get a letter from my son Johnie sooner than I would get one from him, you would very much oblige me by dropping me a few lines communicating to me the most material part of this letter.

I hope you and the ladies of your family will accept of my kindest respects, and I ever am, with esteem,

Dear Madam, your affectionate, humble servant,

Flora Macdonald.

P.S.— Please direct to me, to Mrs. Macdonald, late of Kingsborrow, South Uist, by Dunvegan.

To Mrs. Mackenzie of Delvine, by Dunkeld.

The second reads:—

Milton, 3rd July, 1782.

Dear Madam,—I received your agreeable favour a fortnight ago, and I am happy to find that your health is not worse than when I left you. I return you my most sincere thanks for your being so mindful of me as to send me the agreeable news about Johny's arrival, which relieved me of a great deal of distress, as that was the first accounts I had of him since he sailed. I think, poor man, he has been very lucky for getting into bread so soon after landing. I had a letter from John which, I suppose, came by the same conveyance with yours. I am told by others that it will be in his power now to show his talents, as being in the engineer department. He speaks feelingly of the advantages he got in his youth, and the good example showed him, which I hope will keep him from doing anything that is either sinful or shameful.

I received a letter from Captain Macdonald, my husband, dated from Halifax, the 12th Nov. '81. He was then recovering his health, but had been very tender for some time before. My son, Charles, is captain in the British Legion, and James a lieutenant in the same. They are both in New York. Ranald is captain of Marines, and was with Rodney at the taking of St. Eustati. As for my son Sandy who was amissing I had accounts of his being carried to Lisbon, but nothing certain, which I look upon, on the whole, as a hearsay; but the kindness of Providence is still to be looked upon, as I have no reason to complain, as God has been pleased to spare his father and the rest. I am now in my brother's house, on my way to Skye, to attend my daughter, who is to ly-in in August. They are all in health at present. As for my health at present, it's tolerable, considering my anxious mind and distress of times.

It gives me a great deal of pleasure to hear such good accounts of young Mr. Mackenzie. No doubt he has a great debt to pay who represents his worthy and amiable uncle. I hope you will be so good as remember me to your female companions. I do not despair of the pleasure of seeing you once more, if peace was restored; and I am, dear Madam, with respect and esteem, your affectionate friend,

Flora Macdonald.

CHAPTER 9

Her Husband Returns

When peace was eventually restored, Flora's husband was liberated from Halifax jail, and he made as little delay as possible in returning to Skye, as captain on half-pay. On his arrival at Portree, he was met by his affectionate wife, and a numerous party of friends, to welcome him. He made no delay in reaching Kingsburgh, which, during his absence in America, was left open for his return. For eight or nine years Flora and her husband lived comfortably and happily in their old residence, until both were removed by death, within less than two years of each other. On the 5th of March, 1790, the ever-memorable Flora departed this life. She died of a short illness, nearly two years before her husband. She retained to the last that vivacity of character, and amiableness of disposition, by which she was all her life-time distinguished.

Her death did not take place at her own residence of Kingsburgh, but at Peinduin, a friend's house on the sea coast, about three miles further north. She went thither in her usual health, to pay a friendly visit to the family at Peinduin, where she was taken suddenly ill with an inflammatory complaint, which refused to yield to all the medical skill available at the time. She possessed all her mental faculties to the very last, and calmly departed in the presence of her husband and two daughters.

Such is an imperfect sketch of the history of this distinguished and noble-minded woman, and of her romantic adventures in assisting Prince Charles Edward to effect his escape. To read the accounts of her generous and devoted attachment to the lost cause of the last representative of Scotland's ancient kings, is more like the creation of fiction than a tale of sad reality. She now sleeps calmly by the side of him whom in life she honoured with her heart, and on whom, for about forty years, she had lavished all the wealth, and all the generous impulses of a truly noble and loving heart. And even still her character and virtues lead hundreds from all quarters of the kingdom to her lonely shrine, where they can silently muse upon her goodness, and realise the poet's estimate of woman:—

Honoured be woman, she beams on our sight,
Graceful and fair, like a being of light,
She scatters around her, wherever she strays,
Roses of bliss on our thorn-covered ways—
Roses of Paradise sent from above,
To be gathered and twined in a garland of love.

Flora's remains were shrouded in one of the sheets in which the prince had slept at the mansion of Kingsburgh. With this sheet she never parted in all her travels. It was religiously and faithfully pre-served by her in North Carolina, during the Revolutionary War. She had it in safe keeping even when her own person was in danger. At length the purpose she indended it for was accomplished, when all that was mortal of herself was wrapt in it by her sorrowing family. Her remains were conveyed under shade of night from Peinduin to Kingsburgh. The coffin was carried shoulder-high by a party of stal-wart youths procured for the purpose. One of the party was old John Macdonald, who died at Edinburgh, in 1835, in the house of his son, Donald Macdonald, pipe maker to the Highland Society of Scotland. (John has been already referred to; and his history is recorded in the *Celtic Magazine*.)

Old John related to me very minutely the adventures of that night. He graphically described the storm, which was dreadful! The night was pitch-dark, except when the frequent flashes of lightning spread a momentary gleam over the scene. The thunder rolled with terrific peals; the rain fell in gushing torrents. It would seem as if the ghosts and hobgoblins had that night left their dark abodes to take a " dan-der" abroad, to lash up the elements into a perfect fury!

At that time there were no roads or bridges in Skye, now so well supplied with both. When the funeral party arrived at the river of Hinisdale, about half the journey, it was swollen from bank to bank. The usual ford was impracticable, while higher up it was, if possible, worse. Some proposed to return, while others objected, stating that she whose body they carried never flinched when alive, from any duty which she had undertaken, neither would they flinch from perform-ing their last duties to her mortal remains. After due consultation, it was agreed to attempt crossing by the strand near the sea beach, which was fortunately effected in safety. Shortly after they reached Kingsburgh, where the body lay in state for nearly a week.

At length the funeral day arrived. The procession started at an early hour, as the distance between Kingsburgh and the place of burial was about sixteen miles. The body was interred in the churchyard of Kilmuir, in the north end of Skye, within a square piece of coarse wall, erected in 1776, to enclose the tombs of the Kingsburgh family. The spot is about a mile and a half from the rock called Gailico, near Monkstadt, on which the prince landed in Skye from the Long Island.

The funeral cortege was immense—more than a mile in length—consisting of several thousands of every rank in Skye and the adjacent Isles.

Flora's marriage and funeral, between which there was an interval of forty years, were the most numerously attended of any of which there is any record as having taken place in the Western Isles. Notwithstanding the vast assemblage present, all were liberally supplied with every variety of refreshment. Of genuine "mountain dew" alone upwards of three hundred gallons were served. About a dozen of pipers from the MacCrimmon and MacArthur colleges in Skye, and from other quarters, simultaneously played the "Coronach," the usual melancholy lament for departed greatness.

It must, no doubt, have been consonant with Flora's feelings to have spent her latter years, and breathed her last moments, in that romantic Isle where she had found shelter for her wandering prince, and where she had passed so many of her juvenile years, in the enjoyment of its sublime scenery.

Enough has been said to show that it is from characters such as hers that we have living examples of that self-denying heroism, in perils and privations, that shed a glory over the fidelity and devotedness of the female heart. Tried even by the highest test of these noble virtues, the memory of Flora Macdonald richly deserves to be kept fresh and green over the length and breadth of the land.

Will it be credited that the dust of one so greatly distinguished should have been allowed to moulder for nearly half a century, without even a rude flag to mark her last resting-place. It is true that a thin marble slab, set in a freestone frame, was provided upwards of forty years ago by her son, Colonel John Macdonald, Exeter; but it was cracked while in the act of being landed, from a vessel, on the seabeach. It was set up in that state beside her grave, but in a few months every fragment of it was carried away by tourists, anxious to have some relic of the famous Flora. The inscription on it was as follows:—

> In the family mausoleum at Kilmuir lie interred the remains of the following members of the Kingsburgh family, *viz*:—Alexander Macdonald of Kingsburgh, his son Allan, his sons Charles and James, his son John and two daughters; and of Flora Macdonald, who died in March, 1790, aged 68—a name that will be mentioned in history, and, if courage and fidelity be virtues, mentioned with honour. 'She was a woman of middle stature, soft features, gentle manners, and elegant presence.' So wrote Johnson.

The composition does not forcibly indicate that the schoolmaster was abroad.

In 1834, the grave was opened for the interment of her daughter Anne, Mrs. Major-General Macleod, and even then, after the lapse of forty-four years, several of her bones were quite entire.

A few years ago a costly monument, with an appropriate inscription, was prepared in Inverness for the tomb of the gallant heroine. It is in the form of an Iona Cross—a beautiful, solid monolith of Aberdeen granite, twenty-eight feet high, the design of Alexander Ross, architect, Inverness. The cost was defrayed by public subscriptions. The cross was safely conveyed by steamer, from Inverness to Skye, and erected on a suitable pedestal over the grave. Most unfortunately, however, it did not prove sufficiently substantial to resist the violence of the North wind A severe storm arose, which upset it, and broke it in two! Thus the only real and substantial memorial reared in honour of this justly celebrated woman, has proved abortive, though it has since been partly restored; and what would have been a conspicuous object for centuries, has been ruined through the misapprehension of those who ought to have known better.

Be that as it may, it is fortunate that, should neither sculptural urn nor animated bust be at all reared to the memory of our heroine— that should neither polished granite nor smooth marble ever direct the traveller to her grassy bed, her own unflinching fidelity, and genuine natural virtues, will in all time to come secure for her a more durable monument than the perishable materials of time could possibly ever furnish.

The conduct of Flora Macdonald, alike gallant and romantic, has given rise to various poetical effusions, both in Gaelic and English.

One of the best of these is from the pen of James Hogg, the Ettrick Shepherd; entitled *Flora Macdonald's Lament*. The poem, although purely imaginary, immortalises our heroine's parting with the prince at Portree, and makes her breathe a strain of fervent patriotism in the following strain:—

> Far over yon hills of the heather sae green,
> And down by the corrie that sings to the sea,
> The bonnie young Flora sat sighing her lane,
> The dew on her plaid, and the tear in her ee. S
> he looked at a boat in the breezes that swung,
> Away on the wave, like a bird of the main,
> And aye as it lessened she sighed and she sung—
> Farewell to the lad I shall ne'er see again!
> Farewell to my hero, the gallant and young,
> Farewell to the lad I shall ne'er see again!

> The muircock that crows on the brow of Ben Connel,
> He kens of his bed in a sweet, mossy hame,
> The eagle that soars o'er the cliffs of Clanranald,
> Unawed and undaunted his eyrie can claim.
> The solan can sleep on the shelve of the shore,
> The cormorant roost on his rock of the sea.
> But ah! there is one whose hard fate I deplore,
> Nor house, ha', nor hame in his country has he—
> The conflict is past, and our name is no more—
> There's naught left but sorrow for Scotland and me!

> The target is torn from the arm of the just,
> The helmet is cleft on the brow of the brave—
> The claymore forever in darkness must rust,
> But red is the sword of the stranger and slave.
> The hoof of the horse and the foot of the proud,
> Have trod o'er the plumes on the bonnets of blue;
> Why slept the red bolt in the breast of the cloud,
> While tyranny revell'd in blood o' the true?
> Farewell to my hero, the gallant and good,
> The crown of thy fathers is torn from thy brow.

The unfortunate prince, even under the depression of his latter days, never mentioned the name of his fair protectress but in terms of the highest respect and admiration, though as already stated, he never wrote to her, nor communicated with her in any way, since he parted with her at Portree. Another of our most distinguished Scottish poets has beautifully described the supposed feelings of the prince when reflecting, in after life, upon the services of the gallant Flora. Professor Aytoun made him to say:—

Backwards, backwards, let me wander,
To the noble Northern land;
Let me feel the breezes blowing,
Fresh along the mountain side—
Let me see the purple heather,
Let me hear the thundering tide,
Be it hoarse as Corrievreckan,
Spouting when the storm is high—
Give me but one hour of Scotland,
Let me see it ere I die.
Oh! my heart is sick and heavy,
Southern gales are not for me—
Though the glens are white with winter,
Place me there, and set me free.
Give me back my trusty comrades,
Give me back my Highland Maid—
Nowhere beats the heart so kindly,
As beneath the tartan plaid.
Flora! when thou wert beside me,
In the wilds of far Kintail.
When the cavern gave us shelter,
From the blinding sleet and hail,
When we lurked within the thicket,
And beneath the waning moon,
Saw the sentry's bayonet glimmer,
Heard him chaunt his listless tune;
When the howling storm o'ertook us—
Drifting down the island's lee—
And our crazy bark was whirling,
Like a nutshell on the sea;
When the nights were dark and drear)-,
And amidst the fern we lay,
Faint and foodless, sore with travel,
Waiting for the streaks of day—
When thou wert an angel to me,

Watching my exhausted sleep,
Never did'st thou hear me murmur—
Could'st thou see how now I weep,
Bitter tears and sobs of anguish,
Unavailing though they be—
Oh! the brave! the brave and noble,
That have died in vain for me!

Appendix

(From Mackenzie's *History of the Macdonalds and Lords of the Isles*).

The following are Flora Macdonald's Descendants, so far as we were able to ascertain them, by her marriage with Allan Macdonald, VII. of Kingsburgh:—

1. Charles, a Captain in the Queens' Rangers. At his funeral, Lord Macdonald, on seeing his body lowered into the grave, remarked, "There lies the most finished gentleman of my family and name ". He married Isabella, daughter of Captain James Macdonald of Aird, Troternish, son of William Macdonald, Tutor of Sleat, without issue.

2. Alexander, an Officer in the Naval Service, lost at sea, unmarried. He went down in the *Ville de Paris*, a French line of battleship, taken after a severe fight; he and his brother, Ranald, having been put on board in command of the prize crew.

3. Ranald, a Captain of Marines, "of high professional character, and remarkable for the character of his appearance". He was lost in the *Ville de Paris* with his brother, Alexander, unmarried.

4. James, a brave officer, who served with distinction in Tarlton's British Legion; known in Skye as Captain James Macdonald of Flodigarry. He married Emily, daughter of James Macdonald of Skaebost, with issue, two sons and three daughters—(1) James Somerled Macdonald, Lieutenant-Colonel of the 45th Madras Native Infantry, who died in London, in January, 1842, unmarried. He was buried at Kensal Green Cemetery. (2) Allan Ranald, a Captain in the 4th Bengal Native Infantry, who married Miss Smith, daughter of General Smith, of the Bengal Army, with issue—a son and two daughters. The son, Reginald Somerled Macdonald, of the Colonial Office, died four years ago. He married a daughter of Sir William Grove, an English judge, with issue—two daughters, one of whom, remarkable for her great beauty,

died young in Florence; the other, Zeila Flora Macdonald, married Marshal Canrobert, of France, with issue—several children.

Of the three daughters of Captain James of Flodigarry, two, Flora and Charlotte, died young and unmarried j the former in her father's house at Flodigarry, through an illness brought on by sleeping in damp sheets; the latter, at the age of seventeen, while on a visit to her maternal aunt, the late Mrs. Alexander Mackenzie of Letterewe. Jessie, then only surviving daughter of Captain James Macdonald of Flodigarry, married Ninian Jeffrey, New Kelso, Lochcarron, with issue—eight sons and two daughters; (1) Captain James (died in 1875), who married Mary Irwin, leaving issue—one daughter, who married Dixon Irwin, shipowner, Liverpool; (2) Captain George, of H.M. 32nd Light Infantry, whose career as a soldier was marked by the most reckless bravery.

Before he was seventeen he held a Lieutenant's commission in Don Pedro's army in Portugal. The Portuguese war over, he was next found fighting under General Sir de Lacy Evans, and greatly distinguished himself at the Battle of Venta Hill, on the 5th of May, 1836, when he had to be carried off the field with three bullets in his body. He subsequently obtained a commission in the British army, and, after serving in the tropics, fought through the Sikh war of 1 848-9; was present at the siege and storming of Mooltan, and at the closing battle of Goojerat. He married Annie, daughter of Colonel William Geddes, H.E.I.C.S., with issue—John Macdonald, in the 24th Regiment, and three daughters, one of whom, Flora Macdonald Wylde, died in infancy; Jessie, still unmarried; and Georgina Amelia, who married John Abernethy Rose, merchant, Kurrachee, India.

Captain George Jeffrey died in China in 1868. (3) William John, stipendiary magistrate at Demerara, married Sophia, widow of the Rev. William Hamilton, Rector of the Episcopal Church at Leguan, Essiquibo, Demerara, with issue—two children, a boy and a girl; died in infancy; (4) Allan Ranald Macdonald, a well-known litterateur in London, who married, and has issue, one son, Allan Ninian Charles Macdonald; (5) Thomas Mackenzie, lost at sea, young and unmarried; (6) Alexander Lachlan, in Edinburgh, unmarried; (7) Ninian, and (8) John, both of whom died in infancy. The daughters were, Amelia Macdonald, who died unmarried in 1864; and Agnes Johanna, who married Ranald Livingston of Drimsynie, Argyleshire, with issue— Ranald J. Macdonald, Alexander William John, Emily Nina, Mary Frances, and Flora Charlotte Macdonald. Mr. Livingstone died on the

8th of October, 1871.

5. John, the last survivor of Flora Macdonald's distinguished sons, became Lieutenant-Colonel of the Royal Clan Alpine Regiment, and Commandant of the Royal Edinburgh Artillery. He wrote extensively on military subjects, and was admitted a Fellow of the Royal Society. He married, first, in India, Mrs. Bogle, a widow, and daughter of General Salmon, with issue—two children, who died young. He married, secondly, Frances Maria, eldest daughter of Sir Robert Chambers, Chief Justice of the Supreme Court of Judicature, Bengal, with issue—seven sons and two daughters; (1) Robert, a Major in the Indian army, married, leaving issue—one son, Somerled, who died young; (2) John, a Captain in the Indian army, married, with surviving issue—a son and daughter; (3) Allan, died young; (4) William Pitt, a Major-General in the Indian army, twice married, with surviving issue—seven sons and six daughters, most of whom are married, with issue; (5) Charles Edward, in the Indian Civil Service, married, with issue—a son and daughter, both married; (6) James, a Captain in the Indian army, married, with issue—a son and daughter, both married; (7) Reginald, Lieutenant, 17th Lancers, married Miss Morris, with issue—one daughter, unmarried; (8) Flora Frances, who married Edward Wylde, of the Royal Navy, whom she survives—without issue; she resides at Cheltenham, and is the only living grandchild of the famous Flora Macdonald. (9) Henrietta Louisa Lavinia, who married Benjamin Cuff Greenhill of Knowle Hall, Somersetshire, with issue— three daughters, the eldest of whom, Lavinia, married Edward Amphlett, and died, leaving issue—a son and daughter. The second, Flora, married Thomas Hussey, and is left a widow, with a son and three daughters. The third, Clari, married, without issue.

Colonel John Macdonald died at Exeter, on the 16th of August, 1831, aged 72 years.

6. Anne, who married Major Alexander Macleod of Lochbay, Isle of Skye, and of Glendale, Moore County, U.S.A. He fought through the American War of Independence; subsequently distinguished himself in the European wars, and rose to the rank of Major-General in the British army. His wife, Anne, daughter of Flora Macdonald, survived him, and died at the house of their daughter, Mary, at the village of Stein, Isle of Skye, in 1834. The issue of this marriage was; (1) Norman, killed by Glengarry in a duel, after a quarrel at a Northern Meeting Ball at Inverness; (2 and 3) sons, one of whom married in

India; (4) Flora, who married Mr. MacKay, Forres, with issue; (5) Mary, who died a few years ago, unmarried, in Stein, Isle of Skye.

7. Frances or Fanny, who married Lieutentant Donald Macdonald of Cuidrach, Isle of Skye, with issue.

★★★★★★

Mrs. Major Alexander Macleod, daughter of Flora Macdonald, had a daughter married to Mr. Macdonald of Cuidrach. A daughter named Janet, of said parents, was married to Major Alexander Macdonald of Monkstadt, in the parish of Kilmuir in Skye, and proprietor then of the small property of Courthill, parish of Lochcarron. Major Alexander Macdonald of Monkstadt, had two sons, Hugh and Alexander, and two daughters, Elizabeth and Alice. Hugh was tacksman of Monkstadt, and was married to a daughter of Donald Macdonald of Tanera, afterwards of Kingsburgh, and was proprietor of Skaebost and Stein until sold. Said Hugh Macdonald of Monkstadt had a numerous family of sons and daughters; Alexander, Donald, John, Hugh, James, and daughters—Margaret Bosville, who married a Mr. Todd, proprietor of Underwood, Dumfriesshire, by whom she had a numerous family; Jessie Julia; Johanna, and Eliza, Almost all went to Australia. Alexander, eldest son of Major Macdonald of Monkstadt, was never married. He became insane when a young man by an operation performed on his ears for deafness, and lived principally with his brother Hugh, and was quite harmless. Elizabeth, daughter of Major Alexander Macdonald, was married to Captain Alexander Macleod of Borlin, but had no issue, and her sister Alice was married to Dr. Millar, of Stornoway, with issue. Mrs. Major Macleod had a daughter named Fanny, but I think she was never married."—Rev. Alexander Macgregor, M.A.

★★★★★★

8 and 9. A boy and girl, who died young of typhus fever, aged respectively eleven and thirteen years, at Killiegray, their father's residence when in America, on the borders of Richmond and Montgomery Counties. The present proprietor of the property on which they are buried has, much to his honour, fenced in the graves of these children, to preserve the spot sacred to Flora Macdonald's offspring.

VIEW FROM BEINN, NA. CAILLICH IN SKYE

Flora Macdonald in America

FLORA MACDONALD

Contents

'Mid the pomp of huge London her heart still was yearning
For her home in the corrie, the crag, and the glen;
Though fair be the daughters of England, the fairest
And stateliest walks in the land of the Ben.

To
ANGUS WILTON McLEAN, Esq.
of
LUMBERTON, NORTH CAROLINA
Whose ancestors bore an important part in the scenes
wherein Flora MacDonald was a chief actor in North
Carolina and who takes a deep interest in all things per-
taining to that event, as well as those relating to the Highlands of Scotland and his own distinguished clan, besides
being busily engaged in the practice of law and the de-
velopment of the natural resources of his native State, this
volume is respectfully dedicated by
The Author

HIGHLAND ARMS

FLORA MACDONALD

CHAPTER 1

Introductory Note

Flora MacDonald needs no introduction to all true lovers of Highland Scotch history. It is superfluous to pass a eulogium on her character, or sing her praises. She lives, and will continue to live in the hearts of all who are able to appreciate disinterested heroism of an exalted type. Her countrymen had just been defeated while engaged in the greatest act of chivalry the world had ever witnessed. It was befitting that a woman of true nobility of character should be called on to bear a part, daring, heroic, and romantic. Her character has been extolled; her praises embalmed in song; her heroism depicted as an example to be imitated, and her patriotism to be admired. Withal, a person to be loved for her womanly virtues, which must be regarded as a just pattern of excellence.

The admiration and esteem for Flora MacDonald are largely due to an act on her part which took place between June 26 and 30, 1746, when, at a critical period, she saved Prince Charles Edward from falling into the hands of his enemies. Even a stranger story remains here to be told. Her act at the age of twenty-four, embellished in story and song, has long overshadowed a greater and more deliberate heroism performed at the ripe age of fifty-four. This has been passed over, or else referred to only incidentally. Flora MacDonald was a greater power and a more commanding figure during her residence in America than when she displayed her heroism by saving the life of him who brought countless woes upon her countrymen and hurled many valiant souls down to destruction.

Yet how little is known of Flora MacDonald in America! The fugitive articles and biographical notices of her in the press of her native country betray almost a total ignorance on the subject. Even her biography, written by her granddaughter, Mrs. Flora Frances Wilde, extending to nearly four hundred pages, two-thirds of which is pure fiction, passes over this interesting period with a notice of less than four pages. *The Life of Flora MacDonald*, written by Rev. Alexander Macgregor, and is, as seen, the first part of this book, more conscientious and painstaking biographer, contains but five pages relating to her sojourn in America.

Having seen no satisfactory account of Flora MacDonald's life in North Carolina, I was moved to make a thorough investigation, the result of which I published in the *Celtic Monthly*, Glasgow, for the year 1900. By request of the editor of the *American Monthly Magazine*, I abridged the account, and the same appears in the issue of that journal for August, 1900. Then I dismissed the subject from my mind with no thought of ever pursuing it again.

By special invitation, on the morning of February 20, 1909, I entered the hospitable mansion of Hon. Angus W. McLean, Lumberton. North Carolina, to pay him a visit. Within less than an hour after my appearance, complete arrangements had been entered into, by which I was to rewrite my production on Flora MacDonald, and Mr. McLean was to finance the enterprise. I had no hesitancy on entering into the compact, because I knew that North Carolina contained a very large Highland Scotch population, where the name of Flora MacDonald is venerated, to say nothing of a similar people scattered throughout the various States of the Union, besides the same race in Canada. As these people take a just pride in their ancestry it was safe to infer that the publication would receive a hearty welcome.

It was but a natural consequence that Mr. McLean should be specially interested in Flora MacDonald. His great-grandfather, John MacLean, emigrated from the Isle of Mull to North Carolina, and the clan of MacLean, of that period, was still a strong partisan of the House of Stuart. Besides this, Mr. McLean's great-grandfather, Colonel James MacQueen, was a grandnephew of the heroine of this story, and came to North Carolina, from the Isle of Skye, in the year 1765, accompanied by his sisters, Polly, Nepsie, and Isabel. He landed at Wilmington, proceeded up the Cape Fear River to Cross Creek, where he remained for a short time, and then, with his sisters, went to Anson County, and there taught school for several years.

He was living in that county when Flora MacDonald came to America, and through his influence Allen and Flora MacDonald were persuaded to leave Cameron's Hill and settle in Anson County. Flora lived for a short time with the MacQueen's before settling at Killiegrey. Just after the close of the Revolution, Colonel MacQueen married Nancy MacRae, and purchased a large tract of land about ten miles south of Maxton, giving his home the name of Queensdale, which it still retains. He was a frequent visitor at Flora MacDonald's, and during her hours of adversity, supplied her with money and looked after her necessities while her husband was a prisoner. When Flora left America for Skye, he again supplied her with money to meet her expenses and pressing obligations. He had been successful in amassing what, at that time, was a large fortune.

It is only fair to state that some points in the narrative I found myself unable to unravel. I notified Mr. McLean, who at once gave his time and energy and succeeded in gaining valuable information, and placed the same at my disposal. I further state the manuscript of this work was not submitted to his inspection, and the contents are wholly on my own responsibility.

Before leaving North Carolina, I set about securing all available information, visited Cross Creek (now Fayetteville), sought out those supposed to have items of interest, and from all, living in different communities, I received the utmost courtesy.

The object of this production is not to present the life of Flora MacDonald, but mainly to confine the account to her history as connected with North Carolina, though recognising the necessity for a brief historical sketch in order that a uniform narrative may be maintained. In presenting this testimony, with the additional facts revealed, it is hoped that the effort will meet the approval of all who are interested in the life and character of the Scottish heroine. If such shall be the result, then I shall feel well repaid for my labour.

Franklin, Ohio, April 6, 1909.

CHAPTER 2

Financial Embarrassment of Allen MacDonald

It must have been a matter of common notoriety that Allen Mac-Donald was greatly embarrassed financially. Boswell speaks of it as no secret, and refers to it in the following language:

> In reality my heart was grieved, when I recollected that Kingsburgh was embarrassed in his affairs, and intended to go to America.

This arose from no mismanagement or extravagance of his own or that of his prudent wife, but from the heavy losses of his father, growing out of the troublous times and the part he took in it. The losses appear to have been very great. As the representative of his father, Allen became entangled, but in the face of all his endeavours to surmount the liabilities he found his efforts would prove futile.

The estate, known as Kingsburgh, was a part of the domain of Sir Alexander MacDonald of the Isles, and was occupied by the chamberlain. The first Kingsburgh was James MacDonald, brother of Donald Gorm MacDonald of Sleat, Lord of the Isles, who lived during the times of James V. and Queen Mary. He was succeeded by his son, John, who was killed at the Battle of Lichd Li, fought by nearly the whole clan against the MacLeans of Mull. Allen was the seventh and last of Kingsburgh.

The removal to America was deliberately considered by Allen and Flora, and the conclusion was probably arrived at by the spirit of emigration that had seized the MacDonalds.

CHAPTER 3

Flora MacDonald Removes to America

America had long sought emigrants from Europe, and some of the governors of the provinces interested themselves in arranging for such settlers as were seeking new homes. North Carolina had been a tempting field. The region of the Cape Fear River presented peculiar attractions. It was a beautiful country, the climate mild, there were the tall pines on the uplands, the bottoms covered with rich canebrakes, an abundance of small game, and a soil adapted to the general wants. When the Highlanders first noticed the country there is no documentary evidence, but it is positively known that there was a settlement at the head of navigation of the Cape Fear as early as 1729.

There is a tradition that many Highlanders had located on the river immediately after the disastrous rising in 1715. At the time of the arrival of Flora MacDonald the Highland settlements had spread beyond the Cape Fear, and as high up as the confluence of the Deep and Haw, and to the Pedee where the Yadkin and Uwharie came together, and embraced the present counties of Cumberland, Harnett, Moore, Montgomery, Anson, Richmond, Robeson, and Scotland, and even entering beyond the State line into South Carolina.

The greatest migration was that immediately following the Battle of Culloden, in 1746, led by Neill McNeill, of Jura, the people having been driven from their homes by oppression. These emigrants were of the very best types, well formed, strong, enterprising, and deeply religious. Previous to this time, in 1739, Neill had brought, principally from Argyleshire, three hundred and fifty, and settled them on the Cape Fear. Great numbers of families, during the years 1746 and 1747, came to North Carolina, and settled about Cross Creek (now Fayette-

143

ville) in Cumberland County. There was a North Carolina mania for emigration which pervaded all classes, from the poorest crofter to the well-to-do farmer, and men of easy competence, who were, according to an appropriate song of the day, "Dol a dh'iarruidli an fhortain do North Carolina."

The emigration to America from the Highlands of Scotland was so pronounced that the Scottish papers made frequent reference to it and bemoaned the prevalence. The *Scots Magazine* for September, 1769, records that the ship *Molly* sailed from Islay on August 21, full of passengers for North Carolina, which was the third emigration from Argyle "since the close of the late war." A subsequent issue of the same paper states that fifty-four vessels full of emigrants from the Western Islands and other parts of the Highlands sailed for North Carolina between April and July, 1770, conveying twelve hundred emigrants. Early in 1771, the same magazine states that five hundred emigrants in Islay and adjoining isles were preparing to sail for America.

Again it records that the ship *Adventure* sailed from Loch Erribol, Sunday, August 17, 1772, with upwards of two hundred emigrants from Sutherlandshire for North Carolina. Other reports might be referred to. In 1772 the great MacDonald emigration commenced, and continued until the outbreak of the American Revolution. It was during this period that the MacDonalds outnumbered any of the other clans in North America. The Revolution stopped emigration, which did not break out again until 1805.

The emigrants maintained their manners, customs, language, and religion, all of which have now changed, except their religion, which has been modified. A person passing through the North Carolina country inhabited by the Scotch Highlanders would have seen many a warrior who had fought at Preston, at Falkirk, and at Culloden. He was still the plaided warrior, though his claymore was sheathed.

The MacDonald emigration swept Allen and Flora MacDonald into its current. Flora was ready and willing to sacrifice everything for her husband's comfort, and to accompany him to any quarter where he might surmount his difficulties. In making their domestic arrangements, the son, John, was placed under the care of Sir Alexander Mac-Kenzie of Delvin, until he was of age, for an India appointment, and a girl, then nine years of age, was left with friends. The other children accompanied their parents, who set sail on board the *Baliol* from Campbelton, Kintyre, for North Carolina, in the month of August, 1774. They left the—

Land of grey rock and drifting rain,
Of clamorous brook and boisterous main,—
Of treacherous squall and furious gale,
That bend the mast or rend the sail—
Land of green pine and harebell blue,
Of furze and fern of various hue;
Of deep ravine, and cavern hoar;
Of jutting crag and dangerous shore.

Land of the pibroch and the plaid;
Land of the henchman and the raid;
Land of the chieftain and the clan.
Of haughty laird and vassal-man,
Of Kelt, of Gael, of Catheran,
Land of tall cliff and lonely dell,
The eagle's perch, the outlaw's cell;—
Land of the brave, the fair, the good;
Land of the onslaught, foray, feud;
Land of the ptarmigan and roe;
Land where Glenlivat's fountains flow,
Sparkling and bright as 'mountain dew,'
The heart to warm, the strength renew.
Land of the long, long wintry night,
The dancing, streaming boreal light;
The misty morn, the brightening noon.
The dewy eve, the radiant moon;
Land of the sprightly reel and glee;
The wraith, the fairy, the banshee;
Land where the patriot loves to roam
Far distant from his native home;
And yet, on every foreign strand,
Still sighing for his native land!

Land of basaltic rock and cave,
Where tempests howl and surges rave;
Where Fingal sat and Ossian sung.
While Staffa's echoing caverns rung
With feats achiev'd by heroes' arms.
With tragic tales and war's alarms.
With lover's vows and lady's charms.
Land of the heathery hill and moor.

Of rude stone cot and cold clay floor;
Of barefoot nymph and tartan'd boor.

Land of the kirk, austere and pure.
From pope and prelacy secure,—
With pastor grave and flock demure.
Land of the metaphysic strife,
Where mortal's lot in future life
Is settled by presumptuous man,
Who dares the Almighty's ways to scan!

Land of the eagle's airy nest,
On Glencoe's cliffs or Nevis' crest;
Land of the lochs, that winding sweep
Round mountain's base and headland steep.
Land of the tottering keep and tower,
O'er moat that frown, o'er surge that lower:
Land of the thousand isles that sleep
'Twixt lowering cloud and murmuring deep:
Land of the thousand barks that ride
O'er curling wave or confluent tide;
And, without aid of oar or sail.
Urge their fleet course 'gainst tide or gale.

Land where the torrents leap from high.
And o'er their rocky barriers fly
In sheets of foam, with thundering roar,
Down through the dark ravine to pour;
Land-but the signal gives to weigh;
The wind and tides brook no delay.
Bleak Mull, farewell! I must away.

What were the thoughts of Flora MacDonald as she caught the
last glimpse of Skye, or how deep was the poetic part of her nature,
we will never know. It may be she thought the sentiment, if not the
language of the poet:

Farewell, lovely Skye, sweet isle of my childhood,
Thy blue mountains I'll clamber no more;
Thy heath-skirted corries, green valleys and wildwood,
I now leave behind for a far-distant shore.
Adieu, ye stern cliffs, clad in old, hoary grandeur;
Adieu, ye still dingles, fond haunts of the roe.

How painful to part from the misty-robed Coollin,
The Alps of Great Britain, with antlered peaks high;
Bold Glamaig, Coruisk, and sublime Scuirnagillin,
Make mainland grand mountains look dull, tame, and shy.
Majestic Quiraing, fairy place of Nature,
Stormy Idrigill, Hailleaval, and cloud-piercing Stoer,
And the shining Spar-cave, like some beacon to heaven,
All I deeply lament, and may never see more!

Once more, dearest isle, let me gaze on thy mountains.
Once more let the village church gleam on my view;
And my ear drink the music of murmuring fountains,
While I bid to my old and my young friends adieu.
Farewell, lovely Skye, lake, mountain, and corrie;
Brown isle of the valiant, the brave, and the free;
Ever green to thy sod, resting-place of my Flora,
My sighs are for Skye, my tears are for thee."

The good ship *Baliol* had a very favourable passage to the Western World. The time of the departure of Flora MacDonald was known to her kindred and countrymen in North Carolina, where she was anxiously expected and joyfully received on her arrival. Her name was as well known among them as it was in Scotland, and held in just as great esteem. Many had known her in childhood and early womanhood, though some had not seen her since the rising of 1745. All these people, and others, felt proud of the prospect that she should cross the ocean to become one of their number.

A royal welcome was determined upon, which was actuated by a genuine feeling of love, admiration, and praise for her heroism and noble character. Demonstrations, on a large scale, were made to welcome her to America, and her new home, wherever she might decide to become a denizen. Soon after her landing a largely-attended ball was given in her honour at Wilmington, when she was greatly gratified by the special attention bestowed on her daughter, Anne, then entering into womanhood, and of surpassing beauty.

From Wilmington the Kingsburgh family proceeded to Cross Creek, then regarded as the capital of the Highland settlement. Before reaching Cross Creek the party was met by a large procession in order that Flora might be properly escorted into their midst. As she approached the capital, the strains of the *piobaireachd*, and the martial airs of her native land fell upon the ears of the multitude. In the vast concourse of people were some of her old neighbours and kins-folks, many of whom had crossed the Atlantic years before. Their faces, manner, and voices bore testimony to the welcome of the heart. Many families of distinction pressed upon her to make their dwellings her home, but she respectfully declined, preferring a settled abode of her own.

As the Laird of Kingsburgh had decided to become a planter, he left his family in Cross Creek until he had secured a permanent loca-tion. The house in which the family is said to have lived during this period was built immediately upon the brink of the creek, and for many years after was known as "Flora MacDonald's house," although during my brief visit there four different spots were pointed out as being the site of her residence. It is possible that the various places are remembered from the fact that she was there entertained. During her stay she visited and received visits from her friends, one of whom was Mrs. Rutherford, afterwards Mrs. McAuslin, who, at that time, lived in a house known as the "Stuart Place," north of the Presbyterian Church. Here she saw a painting which represented "Anne of Jura," assisting the prince to escape. "Turn the face of that picture to the wa'," she said. "Never let it see the light again. It belies the truth of history. Anne of Jura was na' there, and did na' help the bonnie prince."

A large number of MacDonalds, principally from Skye and Raasay, and kinsmen of Kingsburgh, had settled northwest of Cross Creek, a distance of twenty miles, about a hill some six hundred feet in height, now called Cameron's Hill, but then known as Mount Pleasant. Here Kingsburgh purchased a large tract of land, the record of the deed is still preserved in the court-house at Fayetteville. Hard by are the sources of Barbaque Creek, and not many miles down the stream stood the old kirk, where the clansmen worshipped, and where Flo-ra inscribed her name on the roll of membership. This church, with that called Longstreet (where Flora also at times worshipped) appears to have been founded in 1758 by Rev. James Campbell, a native of Campbelton, Argyleshire, Scotland. But at the time of Flora's arrival the churches were served by Rev. John McLeod.

Having been persuaded by Colonel MacQueen, Allen disposed of his estate and removed farther west, and, in January, 1776, purchased of Caleb Touchstone a tract of land numbering 550 acres, then in Anson County, but now forming a part of Richmond. The plantation is located eighteen miles north of Rockingham, two miles north of Capel's Mills, on Mountain Creek, and about five miles north of Ellerbe Springs. Allen named the estate Killiegrey, which contained a dwelling and out-houses, which were more pretentious than was then customary among Highland settlers. The outlay cost him four hundred and sixty pounds. The new home was situated in the heart of the pinery region, and in every direction the great pine forest stretched forth. Here the Kingsburgh family immediately established itself, and Flora felt assured that with her family she would spend her remaining days in peace and happiness. Flora and Allen, her husband, were the most commanding figures among all the Highlanders in North Carolina. Their influence was everywhere felt and acknowledged. The power for good was placed in their hands, and wisdom would have suggested that in wielding it a conservative policy should be pursued.

BARBAQUE CREEK KIRK

Chapter 4

Rising of the Highlanders in 1776

The dreams of Flora MacDonald of peace, happiness, and prosperity were doomed to a rude awakening. Before she was well settled in her new home the storm of the American

Revolution burst upon her in all its fury. That she was partially responsible for the final disaster that accomplished the complete financial ruin of the family is beyond question; for she was an active participant in arousing the Highlanders to resistance. Without any hesitation she used her powerful influence in forcing the insurrection of 1776. Notwithstanding this, the disaster would not have overtaken the family had Kingsburgh refrained from precipitating himself into the conflict needlessly and recklessly. His age and past experience should have influenced his course, and bade him remain a silent spectator of the conflict. With blind fatuity he took the wrong side in the struggle, and even then, by the exercise of patience he might have overcome the effects of his folly.

The British authorities bent on the subjugation of the Thirteen Colonies, looked to the formidable Highland Scotch settlements along the Cape Fear and the Mohawk for assistance. The frightful atrocities following the disaster on Drummossie Muir, and the relentless persecution of the Highland clans did not wean that hardy race from the merciless hand of the victor. The American Revolution found all Scotland its pitiless foe. Petition after petition went up from city, town, and hamlet to George III., expressing intense feelings against the Americans, and all protesting that the respective petitioners were the most loyal subjects. Over seven thousand Highlanders, born in Scotland, fought against Washington and his compatriots.

The records demonstrate that the emigrants from the Highlands were received with open arms by the colonists and rendered every assistance needed. Some of the emigrants were destitute even of the means of procuring assistance. Even after the call to armed resistance had been obeyed, a shipload of Highlanders was stranded in Virginia, and every care was rendered by the colonists.

On the breaking out of hostilities, the Highlanders became an object of consideration to the contending parties. They were numerically strong, increasing in numbers, and their military qualities second to none. British emissaries were sent among all of them, though it was known that their inclination strongly favoured the royal cause, and that side left no means untried to cement their loyalty, even to appeals to their religious natures. To counteract the efforts of the royalists the Americans were at a great disadvantage, because it was impossible for them to secure a Gaelic-speaking minister, clothed with authority to go among them. Even the resources and loyalty of Rev. James Campbell would be counteracted by Rev. John McLeod, because he stood nearer to the MacDonalds and MacLeods, the two dominant clans. His sympathies were thrown against the Americans, and his actions were of such a nature that it was deemed prudent to arrest him, but he was discharged on May 11, 1776.

No steps were taken by the Americans to enrol the Highlanders into military companies. Their efforts were made to enlist the sympathies of the clansmen. On the other hand, the royal governor, Josiah Martin, took steps to enrol the North Carolina settlers into active British service. The governor was in constant communication with them, and, in a measure, directed their movements. Allen MacDonald of Kingsburgh was the recognised leader. As early as July 3, 1775, he went to Fort Johnson, and there concerted with Governor Martin regarding the raising of a battalion of "good and faithful Highlanders," fully calculating on the recently-settled MacDonalds and MacLeods. Prior communications were held between Martin and Kingsburgh, because the former recommended that the latter should be appointed major, in his communication to Lord Dartmouth, on June 30 preceding.

In the report of the same to the same, dated November 12, 1775, the statement is made that Kingsburgh had raised a company, as had also his son-in-law, Alexander MacLeod. From the official records, it may therefore be seen that the Laird of Kingsburgh was not drawn into the controversy under restraint or under solicitation. How far his early steps in the matter were influenced by his wife. Flora, will never be known ; but, in all probability, he took no action without her knowledge and consent. Whatever view we may take of their action, whether it be censure or praise, it must be admitted that both were governed by their sense of right and justice. It is but fair in judging the motives of every one to put ourselves exactly in the position of the one adjudged. The sense of right, *per se*, is an entirely different thing.

It is not to be presumed that the Provincial Congress of North Carolina, and other patriotic bodies, were not aroused in every particular. We find that the Congress, on August 23, 1775, appointed from among its members Archibald MacLaine, Alexander McAllister, Farquhard Campbell, Alexander McKay, and others, "a committee to confer with the gentlemen who have lately arrived from the Highlands in Scotland to settle in this province, and to explain to them the nature of our unhappy controversy with Great Britain, and to advise and urge them to unite w4th the other inhabitants of America in defence of their rights which they derive from God and the Constitution."

Governor Martin stood ready to precipitate matters and involve the Highlanders in a quarrel with the other inhabitants; for in his letter to Lord Dartmouth, of June 30, 1775, he declares he "could collect immediately among the emigrants from the Highlands of Scotland," "three thousand effective men," and begs permission "to raise a battalion of a thousand Highlanders here," and "I would most humbly beg leave to recommend Mr. Allen MacDonald of Kingsburgh to be major, and Captain Alexd. McLeod of the marines now on half-pay to be first captain, who, besides being men of great worth and good character, have most extensive influence over the Highlanders here, a great part of which are of their own names and families."

On November 12, following, the governor again writes that he can

. . . .assure your lordship that the Scotch Highlanders here are generally and almost without exception staunch to government, and that Captain Alexander McLeod, a gentleman from the Highlands of Scotland and late an officer in the marines, who has been settled in this province about a year and is one of the gentlemen I had the honour to recommend to your lordship to be appointed a captain in the battalion of Highlanders, I proposed with His Majesty's permission to raise here, found his way down to me at this place about three weeks ago, and I learn from him that he is, as well as his father-in-law, Mr. Allen MacDonald, proposed to me for major of the intended corps, moved by my encouragements have each raised a company of Highlanders since which a Major McDonald who came here some time ago from Boston under the orders from General Gage to raise Highlanders to form a battalion, (see MacLean's *Scotch Highlanders in America*), to be commanded by Lieut. Coll. Allan McLean, has made them proposals of being appointed captains in that corps, which they have accepted on the condition that His Majesty does not approve my proposal of raising a battalion of Highlanders and reserving to themselves the choice of appointments therein in case it shall meet with his Majesty's approbation in support of that measure.

The activities of the royalists during the year 1775 were so pronounced as to cause the patriots to be on the alert. For some reason the Highlanders were visited by General Lachlan McIntosh of the Georgia Highlanders, who was born in Badenoch, Scotland, in 1725, but had been in America since the age of eleven. He used every argument in his power to induce his countrymen in North Carolina to remain neutral in the conflict then impending, as it was the only safe and consistent course for them to take. In answer, the agents of Governor Martin appealed to their professions of loyalty, their love of their native country, that all efforts against the king had proved abortive, and that all who resisted the government would be dealt with as were their fathers and brothers after the battle of Culloden, besides reminding them of their oath of allegiance.

Against these delusive arguments General McIntosh reminded them that they had no attachment for the reigning house of Hanover, and there was no inducement to risk anything in maintaining its authority; that they had already suffered severely, on several occasions, by the arbitrary and unjust measures of the present government, and that they need expect nothing better in times to come. He further assured them that if they would remain quietly at home, he had no doubts that he would succeed in procuring their safety and peace. The appeals of McIntosh were so forcible that all consented save a few military characters, some hot-headed young men, and a majority of Clans MacDonald and MacLeod.

Unfortunately, directly after his departure the arrival of Donald McDonald and Donald McLeod, assisted by the Laird of Kingsburgh, overturned the good that had been reached. McDonald was sixty-five years of age, had fought at Culloden and Bunker Hill, and was sent, with McLeod, from Boston, by General Gage, to take command of the Highlanders in North Carolina. They came by way of Newbern, where they were arrested, but pretended that they were wounded at Bunker Hill, and had left the army with the design of settling among their friends. They arrived in June, 1775, and immediately set out on their mission.

The Laird of Kingsburgh early came under the suspicion of the Committee of Safety at Wilmington. On the very day, July 3, 1775, he was in consultation with Governor Martin, its chairman was directed to write to him:

> ...to know from himself respecting the reports that circulate of his having an intention to raise troops to support the arbitrary measures of the ministry against the Americans in this colony, and whether he had not made an offer of his services to Governor Martin for that purpose.

On August 21, 1775, the Provincial Congress began its session at Hillsboro. Cumberland County was represented by Farquhard Campbell, Thomas Rutherford, Alexander McKay, Alexander McAlister, and Daniel Smith. Campbellton sent Joseph Hepburn. Among the members of this Congress having distinctly Highland names, besides those already mentioned, were John Campbell and John Johnston from Bertie, Samuel Johnston of Chowan, Duncan Lamon of Edgecombe, John McNitt Alexander of Mecklenburg, Kenneth McKenzie of Martin, Jeremiah Frazier of Tyrell, William Graham of Tryon, and Archibald Maclaine of Wilmington. One of the acts of this Congress was to divide the State into military districts and the appointment of field officers of the Minute Men. For Cumberland County, Thomas Rutherford was appointed colonel; Alexander McAllister, lieutenant-colonel; Duncan McNeill, first major; Alexander McDonald, second major. One company of Minute Men was to be raised. The act was passed on September 9.

How many proved unfaithful to the interests at first avowed, I am unable to determine. Prominent among those who proved recreant to their trust we find the names of Thomas Rutherford and Farquhard Campbell. The latter dealt treacherously with both sides.

During the year 1775 no overt acts were committed, although in the northern provinces the contest had become bloody, and the Continental Congress had an army besieging Boston. True, military companies had been formed by both contestants, and as late as November and December, 1775, the two parties in Cross Creek mustered on opposite sides of the village, then returned into town and lived in great harmony.

On the Cape Fear were intelligent, public-spirited, and patriotic men who were determined to resist all encroachments, and who became very active in impressing upon the people of their respective neighbourhoods the duty and importance of maintaining their liberties and resisting the oppression of the English government. Among these the most noted were Colonels James Moore, John Ashe, Alexander Lillington, Robert Rowan, and Thomas Robeson.

The early intrigues by the British agents with the Scotch Highlanders were more guessed at than known by the patriots. The early days of 1776 saw the masque torn from the face, and the intrigues reached their culmination. The war party among the Highlanders was greatly in the ascendant. The Americans, while at first they felt anxious, now had their feelings changed to bitterness, owing to the fact that they were not only precipitating themselves into a quarrel in which they had no special cause, but also were exhibiting ingratitude to those who had been their benefactors. Up to this time the Americans had only sought a redress of grievances, and but very few foresaw the ultimate outcome.

True, the Highlanders had viewed the matter from a different standpoint. They failed to realise the craftiness of Governor Martin in compelling all who had recently arrived to take the oath of allegiance, which, with all the sacredness of religion, they felt to be binding. They had ever been taught that all promises were sacred, and a liar was a greater criminal than a thief. Still, it must be granted, they had every opportunity to learn the true status of the situation; independence had not yet been proclaimed; Washington was still in his trenches about Boston, and the Americans continued to petition the British throne to take cognizance of their grievances.

What the Highlanders expected to gain by their proposed actions would be difficult even to conjecture. They certainly failed to realize the condition of the country, and the insuperable difficulties to be overcome before they could make a junction with Sir Henry Clinton. Even should they assemble peaceably in Wilmington, there they would be one hundred miles from their homes and families, who would necessarily be at the mercy of their enemies, who had become bitter on account of their own actions. They were blinded and exhibited a want of ordinary foresight.

There was also an exhibition of reckless indifference of the responsible parties to the welfare of those they had so successfully duped. During all the years which have elapsed since their ill-advised action, though treated with the utmost charity, their bravery applauded, even by their descendants they have been condemned for their rude precipitancy, besides failing to realize the changed condition of affairs, and not resenting the injuries they had received from the House of Hanover that had harried their country and hanged their fathers on the murderous gallows-tree.

Lieutenant Alexander McLean and Donald McLeod had been the trusted agents of Governor Martin to the back counties of North Carolina. They had returned with flattering reports, which he was not slow in transmitting to Sir Henry Clinton. Based partly on these reports, a vigorous campaign was determined on for 1776, the brunt of which was to fall upon North Carolina. The program was for Sir Henry Clinton, with a fleet of ships and seven corps of Irish regulars, to be at the mouth of the Cape Fear early in the year 1776, and there form a junction with the Highlanders and others to be raised from the interior.

Believing that this armament would arrive in January or early in February, Martin made preparations for the revolt; for his "unwearied, persevering agent," Alexander McLean, brought written assurances from the principal persons to whom he had been directed, that between two and three thousand men would take the field at the governor's summons. Under this encouragement McLean was again sent into the back country with a commission dated January 10, 1776, authorising Allen MacDonald, Donald MacDonald, Alexander McLeod, Donald McLeod, Alexander McLean, Allen Stewart, William Campbell, Alexander McDonald, and Neal McArthur, of Cumberland and Anson counties, besides seventeen other persons, not connected with the Highlanders, who resided in a belt of counties in middle Carolina, to raise and array all the king's loyal subjects, and to march them in a body to Brunswick by February 15.

It has been argued because Allen MacDonald of Kingsburgh's name appears first in the list, it was designed by Governor Martin that he should be first in command. This conclusion is not warranted by the facts. Donald MacDonald was sent direct from Boston in order to take military command of the troops, and for several months had been on the ground. He came with the commission of major, and Martin had no authority to issue a higher commission. Besides this, the commission of Donald antedates that of Allen. Martin did commission Donald brigadier-general, but this was unauthorised. Said commission is still in Fayetteville. If Allen had any experience as a military commander the fact has not been recorded in history. He was in hiding for a while after the Battle of Culloden, but this was on account of the arrest of old Kingsburgh, his father.

Upon receiving his orders from Governor Martin, at once General MacDonald issued the following:

By His Excellency Brigadier-General Donald McDonald, Commander of His Majesty's Forces for the time being in North Carolina:

A Manifesto.

Whereas, I have received information that many of His Majesty's faithful subjects have been so far overcome by apprehension of danger as to fly before His Majesty's Army as from the most inveterate enemy ; to remove which, as far as lies in my power, I have thought it proper to publish this Manifesto, declaring that I shall take the proper steps to prevent any injury being done, either to the person or properties of His Majesty's subjects; and I do further declare it to be my determined resolution, that no violence shall be used to women and children, as viewing such outrages to be inconsistent with humanity, and as tending in their consequences to sully the arms of Britons and soldiers.

I, therefore, in His Majesty's name, generally invite every well-wisher to that form of government under which they have so happily lived, and which, if justly considered, ought to be esteemed the best birth-right of Britons and Americans, to repair to His Majesty's Royal Standard, erected at Cross Creek, where they will meet with every possible civility, and be ranked in the list of friends and fellow-soldiers, engaged in the best and most glorious of all causes, supporting the rights and constitution of their country.

Those, therefore, who have been under the unhappy necessity of submitting to the mandates of Congress and committees—those lawless, usurped, and arbitrary tribunals—will have an opportunity (by joining the King's Army), to restore peace and tranquillity to this distracted land—to open again the glorious streams of commerce—to partake of the blessings of inseparable from a regular administration of justice, and be again reinstated in the favourable opinion of their Sovereign.

Donald McDonald.

By His Excellency's command.

Kenn McDonald, P.S.

On February 5, after a conference with the principal leaders, General MacDonald issued another manifesto in which he declares it to be his intention that:

No violation whatever shall be offered to women, children, or private property to sully the arms of Britons or freemen employed in the glorious and righteous cause of rescuing and delivering this country from the usurpation of rebellion, and that no cruelty whatever be offered against the laws of humanity, but what resistance shall make necessary; and that whatever provisions and other necessaries be taken for the troops shall be paid for immediately; and in case any person, or persons, shall offer the least violence to the families of such as will join the Royal Standard, such person or persons may depend that retaliation will be made; the horror of such proceedings, it is hoped, will be avoided by all true Christians.

Manifestos being the order of the day, Thomas Rutherford, erstwhile patriot, deriving his commission from the Provincial Congress, though having alienated himself, but signing himself colonel, also issued one in which he declared that this is:

To command, enjoin, beseech, and require all His Majesty's faithful subjects within the County of Cumberland to repair to the King's Royal Standard, at Cross Creek, on or before the sixteenth, present, in order to join the King's army; otherwise, they must expect to fall under the melancholy consequences of a declared rebellion, and expose themselves to the just resentment of an injured, though gracious sovereign.

On February 1, General MacDonald erected the royal standard at Cross Creek, in the public square, and in order to cause the Highlanders to respond with alacrity, various methods were employed that the military spirit might be freely inculcated.

The call came like an emergency, summoning the disaffected to the standard of the king. To many of the Highlanders it was a slogan, a veritable fiery cross hurled over the sand hills and the pine forests. But there were others who still needed awakening and appeared to realise that danger lurked in the distance. Those holding the minor commissions in the military service found it necessary to become exceedingly active and to use every means and exertion in their power. Efforts were not only made among the Highlanders, but also among the Regulators, who generally sympathized with the British notwithstanding their terrible defeat at the Battle of Alamance on May 16, 1771. The rendezvous of the latter was at Cross Hill, less than two miles from the present town of Carthage, where about five hundred assembled, some of whom, however, were Highlanders. Owing to the fact that the Highland Army moved out of Cross Creek before the time appointed, Colonel William Fields failed to join the command. He was on his way with his regiment, but learning of the defeat at Moore's Creek, returned home.

At Cross Hill the military array was met by General MacDonald, who formally erected the king's standard, and had the governor's proclamation read along with the military commissions which had been given. An organisation was made in due form, so far as was practicable, but the claims for office were too great to be satisfied.

The Scotch were an entirely different people from the Regulators. From time immemorial they had been warlike. If not engaged in contending against a common enemy, they had their training in the conflict of clan against clan. No land of the same territorial limits and the same population abounds more in legendary, traditionary, and historical narratives of hard-fought battles, personal encounters, and perilous adventures. Fortunately, the accounts have been preserved by their bards, a noted class even from the days of Ossian down to the present hour. During the long nights of winter, in Scotland, the tales were rehearsed in various huts where the people would assemble. Then, again, the sound of the *pibroch* would at any time arouse the martial spirit of the people, from the mere lad to the man of great age; for old and young were upon the field of carnage.

At the opening of the campaign of 1776, most of the Highlanders had reached the age of fifty or more, and had imbibed military spirit from infancy, cherished in youth, and exhibited the same in manhood. In America all the legends and tales were taught the youth, just the same as though they were living on the ancient clan lands of Scotland.

The sound of the *pibroch* was now heard in the pine forests of America summoning the clansmen to arms. Nightly balls were inaugurated that the people might assemble and be properly enthused. The war spirit of Flora MacDonald was stirred within her. Night after night she attended these gatherings; addressed the men in their native Gaelic, and urged them to enter the king's army. During the day, on horseback, with her husband, she went from house to house and used her persuasive powers to excite the slow, the indifferent, and doubtful to action. To her personal appeals the success of the gathering was largely due.

According to the *American Historical Review* of 1872, the following letter, written by Flora MacDonald, was preserved in Fayetteville in 1852:

> February 1, 1776.
>
> Dear Maggie: Allan leaves tomorrow to join Donald's standard at Cross Creek, and I shall be alone wi' my three bairns. Canna ye come and stay wi' me awhile? There are troublous times ahead I ween. God will keep the right. I hope all our ain are in the right, prays your good friend,
>
> Flory McDonald.

Other influences of a far different nature were at work. Caruthers, in his *Revolutionary Incidents*, gives an example, in the case of Hugh MacDonald, who declared that General MacDonald and Donald MacLeod persuaded the Scotch "to step forward and draw their broad swords, as their forefathers had often done, in defence of their king, who would give them double wages and double honours."

These gentlemen, notwithstanding their influence among the ignorant Scotch, were instigated by selfish and speculative motives; and not only they, but their subaltern officers also. I well recollect, though only entering on my fourteenth year, that John Martin, who called himself a captain in the contemplated regiment, came to the home of my father, who then lived near the place now known by the name of Carthage, in Moore County; and, after causing him to enlist, told him that he must take me along with him. My father said that I would be of no service in the army as a soldier, and as his wife was a sickly woman and the children all weakly, I would be useful at home to the family. *'Never mind your family,'* was his reply, *'he will count one to procure me a commission, and he will draw you a soldier's pay.'* My father told him that would be unjust. 'If you do not take him with you, I will see you hanged when we see the king,' was his reply to that; and my father was afraid of his threats, knowing that when offended he was not too strict in points of

160

honour. Five days after this they were embodied and marched to Cross Creek.

At length the time arrived for the gathering at Cross Creek. Then the Highlanders were seen coming from near and from far, from the wide plantations on the river bottoms, and from the rude cabins in the depths of the lonely pine forests, with the claymore at their side, in tartan garments and feathered bonnet, and keeping step to the shrill music of the bagpipe. There came, first of all. Clan MacDonald, with Clan MacLeod near at hand, with lesser numbers of Clan MacKenzie, Clan MacRae, Clan MacLean, Clan MacKay, Clan MacLachlan, and still others. There were also about two hundred Regulators. As may be inferred, all who were capable of bearing arms did not respond, because some would not engage in a cause where their traditions and affections had no part, some of whom hid in the swamps and others in the forest.

The number assembled, and which remained with the army, has been variously estimated, the figures running from fifteen hundred to three thousand. Stedman, an officer under Cornwallis, in his *History of the American War,* Vol. I., states "the army of the loyalists consisted of about eighteen hundred men," which I am inclined to think is about correct, though Edmund Burke states that after his defeat General MacDonald admitted he had three thousand.

There appears to be pretty strong evidence that in the host there was division and even conflicting claims and various opinions almost from the commencement of the enterprise to the final overthrow. While at Cross Creek it was found very difficult to organise and arrange the companies, regiments, and precedence of rank so as to give general satisfaction and secure harmonious cooperation. Those who had been militia officers expected to hold the same rank in the army; and, on this principle there were too many officers for the requisite complement of men. The officers, and others who had lately arrived from Scotland, were called "newcomers," and "new Scotch," and looked upon with jealousy by the rest. Those who had been born in this country or had been long residents were unwilling to have the "newcomers" promoted over them.

General MacDonald was forced to exercise all his wisdom and patience in tracing back their family standing and inquiring into their respective qualifications before making a decision. To give entire satisfaction was an impossible task. Some were so highly offended, at what they considered an injustice, and others failing to see such necessary discipline as would be conducive to success, that they withdrew and soon after joined the provincials. Nor was this the only disturbing element, for it had been given out that the governor was at Campbelton with a thousand British regulars to receive them, and this report had accelerated their movements. On approaching their encampment, they saw the statement was without foundation, and large numbers turned their faces homeward. Having thus been deceived, the Regulators lost confidence in all other representations made by their leaders, and in consequence hundreds retired.

Amidst the dissensions and discouragements, Flora MacDonald arose equal to the emergency, and threw the weight of her character, influence, and oratory into the scale. On the public square, near the royal standard, in Gaelic, she made a powerful address, with all her power, exhibiting her genius she dwelt at length upon the loyalty of the Scotch, their bravery, and the sacrifices her people had made. She urged them to duty, and was successful in exciting all to a high military pitch. When she had concluded, the piper asked her what tune he should play. Like a flash she replied, "Give them leather breeches," which was probably suggested by the Scots wearing buckskin breeches, rolled up at the bottoms.

The movements of the Highlanders and Regulators were carefully watched by the patriots, though much had been done in great secrecy; but the passing of armed men could not well be effectually concealed.

Cross Creek had been greatly disturbed for months. In the midst of the loyalists there were a few sterling patriots. Robert Rowan, in the early stages of the movement, had formed an independent company, and determined to find out the action of the community. He was thus early prepared to give notice of what was in motion.

When the hosts began to move to their standards, swift messengers were immediately despatched to give warning to the patriot leaders. At Salisbury the district Committee of Safety met on February 6 and gave orders to the county committees to embody the militia and minute men and send them forward. Three days later the Tryon committee directed that each captain should detail one-third of the effective men in his district and march to suppress the insurrection. Everywhere the country was alarmed and thoroughly aroused. At the west, the forces were collected at Charlotte, Salisbury, and Hillsboro. On the tenth the committee at New Bern directed Colonel Richard Caswell to march immediately, and the colonels of Dobbs, Johnston,

Pitt, and Craven counties were ordered to join Caswell with their troops. The patriot forces in Mecklenberg, Rowan, Granville, Bute, Surry, Guilford, Orange, and Chatham were hurried to the scene of action.

A messenger reached Wilmington on the ninth. Colonel James Moore at once issued orders to prepare to march against the insurgents. For eighty hours there was severe, unremitting labour in making preparations. Colonel Moore moved toward Cross Creek, being joined *en route* by the Bladen militia. Colonel Alexander Lillington and Colonel John Ashe were soon in the field. Nearly nine thousand men were in motion, and all the rest were ready to turn out at a moment's notice. It was determined to crush out the rebellion without delay.

The loyalists of Surry were speedily dispersed. In Guilford, Colonel James Martin assembled the patriots at the "Cross Roads," but the loyalists passed on. A company of which Samuel Devinny, one of the former Regulators, was the head, being opposed by Captain Dent, killed him. It thus appears that Captain Dent was the first in North Carolina to fall in the contest.

The rising of the Highlanders at the time appointed was ill-advised, and showed a want of judgment on the part of Governor Martin. The object of marching the Highlanders to Wilmington was to act in conjunction with a British fleet. At the very moment of the assembling of the Highlanders the fleet was still in Cork, Ireland, and remained there until February 12, and did not arrive at the Cape Fear until May 3. Even if the Highland Army, under the circumstances, had reached Wilmington, it would have fared more disastrously than its defeat at the Widow Moore's Creek Bridge.

Deserted by the Regulators, and the Americans swarming around him. General MacDonald found it to be necessary to take his departure before the time appointed. Stedman, in his *History of the American War,* has pointed out that MacDonald had decided to avoid all conflict, and to gain the sea coast with the least possible cost. That he did not intend to act offensively is proved from the fact that at Rockfish the Americans occupied an unsoldierly position and one that would provoke an attack. On their left was a morass with a deep swamp, the northwest of the river on the right, and the deep creek of the Rockfish to the rear—all of which invited annihilation. This position must have been known to many in MacDonald's army. Then, again, the original position of the Americans at Moore's Creek Bridge was almost equally as dangerous, and if MacDonald had charged on his arrival there, victory would have been easily won.

Fortunately, however, the insecurity of the position did not escape the vigilance of Colonel Caswell, and as soon as night came he retreated over the bridge. The Highland Army at Cross Creek was neither prepared for battle nor for the march, despite all the exertions General MacDonald had put forth. The armament was as good as could be desired under the circumstances and did not lack in baggage and magazine wagons.

On February 18, the Highland Army took up its line of march for Wilmington, and as the regiments filed out of Cross Creek, Flora MacDonald reviewed them from under an oak tree, still standing on Cool Spring Street. Then mounting her snow-white charger, she rode up and down the marching columns, and animated them in the most cheerful manner. She had staked much on that army. There was her husband, Allen, with the rank of major; her son, Alexander, a captain, and her son-in-law, Alexander MacLeod, a colonel. The soldiers were in high glee, and as they passed along, with drums beating, pipes playing, and flags flying, they sang their old Scotch songs and rehearsed the stories of their native land.

South of Cross Creek is a small stream called Rockfish, which flows into Cape Fear River. Two roads lead from Cross Creek to Wilmington, one called the Brunswick road, the other the Negro Head Point Road. The Brunswick Road crosses Rockfish Creek, which was selected by General MacDonald for his route to Wilmington. After marching four miles, General MacDonald went into camp, on account of the American forces in his front.

Flora MacDonald continued with the army until it reached the brow of Haymount, near the site of the old United States Arsenal, where it encamped for one night. In the morning when the army took up the line of march midst banners streaming in the breeze and martial music floating in the air, Flora took her departure.

It was with great difficulty that her husband obtained her consent to return, reasoning that his life was enough to put in jeopardy. Having consented, she embraced her husband, her eyes dimmed with tears, she uttered a fervent prayer for his safety and speedy return to Killiegrey; she mounted her snow-white horse, rode along the columns of the army, encouraging the men, then retraced, and was soon in Cross Creek, accompanied by Malcolm MacKay, aged sixteen. The first night she spent with Mrs. MacKay, Malcolm's mother, near Longstreet. From there she went to Killiegrey, in Anson County, where she remained until the estate was confiscated by the Americans, when she removed to a plantation on Little River belonging to Kenneth Black. This continued to be her residence until she left America. She made frequent visits to Cross Creek until her final removal.

General James Moore, anticipating the movements of the Highland Army, with great celerity moved up the Cape Fear, and took possession of Rockfish bridge, on the fifteenth, and then held the pass and fortified his camp. There he was immediately joined by Robert Rowan with sixty men from Cross Creek, and later by Lillington, Ashe, and Kenan with the Duplin militia, increasing the whole number to fifteen hundred. In the meanwhile, Colonel Thackston and Colonel Alexander Martin were rapidly approaching from the west with still larger re-enforcements.

On the nineteenth the royalists were paraded with a view to assail General Moore on the following night. A bare suspicion that such a prospect was contemplated was a sufficient cause for some of Colton's men to run off with their arms. This condition of affairs alarmed General MacDonald. However, the same day he sent General Moore the following:

Headquarters, February 19, 1776.
Sir: I herewith send the bearer, Donald Morrison, by advice of the Commissioners appointed by his Excellency, Josiah Martin, and in behalf of the army now under my command, to propose terms to you as friends and countrymen. I must suppose you unacquainted with the Governor's Proclamation, commanding all His Majesty's loyal subjects to repair to the king's royal standard, else I should have imagined you would, ere this, have joined the King's army, now engaged in His Majesty's service. I have therefore thought it proper to intimate to you, that, in case you do not, by twelve o'clock tomorrow, join the Royal standard, I must consider you as enemies, and take the necessary steps for the support of legal authority.
I beg leave to remind you of His Majesty's speech to his Parliament, wherein he offers to receive the misled with tenderness and mercy, from motives of humanity. I again beg of you to accept the proferred clemency. I make no doubt but you will show the gentleman sent on this message every possible civility; and you may depend in return, that all your officers and men

which may fall into our hands shall be treated with an equal degree of respect.

I have the honour to be, in behalf of the army, sir, your most obedient, humble servant,

Donald McDonald.

To the Commanding Officer at Rockfish.

P. S. His Excellency's Proclamation is herewith enclosed.

Knowing that Colonel Martin and Colonel Thackston were nearing the neighbourhood, and wishing to gain time. General Moore thus replied to the missive:

Camp at Rockfish, February 19, 1776.

Sir: Yours of this day I have received; in answer to which, I must inform you, that the terms which you are pleased to say, in behalf of the army under your command, are offered to us as friends and countrymen, are such as neither my duty nor inclination will permit me to accept, and which I must presume you too much of an officer to expect of me. You were very right when you supposed me unacquainted with the Governor's Proclamation; but as the terms therein proposed are such as I hold incompatible with the freedom of Americans, it can be no rule of conduct for me.

However, should I not hear further from you before twelve o'clock tomorrow, by which time I shall have an opportunity of consulting my officers here, and perhaps. Colonel Martin, who is in the neighbourhood of Cross Creek, you may expect a more particular answer; meantime, you may be assured that the feelings of humanity will induce mne to show that civility to such of you as may fall into our hands, as I am desirous should be observed towards those of ours who may be unfortunate enough to fall into yours.

I am, sir, your most obedient and very humble servant,

James Moore.

On the succeeding day General Moore sent the following to General MacDonald:

Camp at Rockfish, February 20, 1776.

Sir: Agreeable to my promise of yesterday, I have consulted the officers under my command, respecting your letter, and am happy in finding them unanimous in opinion with me.

We consider ourselves engaged in a cause the most glorious and honourable in the world, the defence of the liberties of mankind, in support of which, we are determined to hazard everything dear and valuable; and in tenderness to the deluded people under your command, permit me, sir, through you, to inform them, before it is too late, of the dangerous and destructive precipice on which they stand, and to remind them of the ungrateful return they are about to make for their favourable reception in this country.

If this is not sufficient to recall them to the duty which they owe to themselves and their posterity, inform them that they are engaged in a cause in which they cannot succeed, as not only the whole force of this country, but that of our neighbouring provinces, is exerting, and now actually in motion to suppress them, and which must end in their utter destruction. Desirous, however, of avoiding the effusion of human blood, I have thought proper to send you a copy of the test recommended by the Continental Congress, which, if they will yet subscribe and lay down their arms, by twelve o'clock tomorrow, we are willing to receive them as friends and countrymen. Should this offer be rejected, I shall consider them as enemies to the constitutional liberties of America, and treat them accordingly.

I cannot conclude without reminding you, sir, of the oath which you and some of your officers took at New Berne, on your arrival in this country, which I imagine you will find difficult to reconcile to your present conduct. I have no doubt that the bearer. Captain James Walker, will be treated with proper civility and respect in your camp.

I am, sir, your most obedient and humble servant,

James Moore,

General MacDonald took occasion to answer the communication of General Moore in the following language:

Headquarters, February 20, 1776.
Sir: I received your favour by Captain James Walker, and observed your declared sentiments of revolt, hostility, and rebellion to the king, and to what I understand to be the constitution of this country. If I am mistaken, further consequences must determine; but while I continue in my present sentiment, I shall consider myself embarked in a cause which must, in its

consequences, extricate this country from anarchy and licentiousness. I cannot conceive that the Scots emigrants, to whom I imagine you allude, can be under greater obligations to this country than to that of England, under whose gracious and merciful government they alone could have been enabled to visit this western region; and I trust, sir, it is in the womb of time to say, that they are not that deluded and ungrateful people which you would represent them to be. As a soldier in His Majesty's service, I must inform you, if you are yet to learn, that it is my duty to conquer, if I cannot reclaim, all those who may be hardy enough to take up arms against the best of Masters, as of Kings.

I have the honour to be, in behalf of the army under my command, sir, your most obedient servant.

Donald McDonald.

To James Moore, Esq.

General MacDonald was fully aware that he could not put his threat into execution, for he had been informed that the minutemen were gathering in swarms around him; that Colonel Caswell at the head of the minute-men of Newbern, nearly eight hundred strong, were marching through Duplin County to effect a junction with General Moore, and that his communications with the seacoast had been cut off. Realising the extremity of his danger, he resolved to avoid an engagement, and leave the army at Rockfish in his rear, and by celerity of movements, and crossing rivers at unexpected places, to disengage himself from the larger bodies and fall upon the command of Colonel Caswell. Before marching he exhorted his men to fidelity, expressed bitter scorn for the "base cravens who had deserted the night before," and concluded by saying:

If any amongst you are so faint-hearted as not to serve with the resolution of conquering or dying, this is the time to declare themselves.

The speech was answered by a general huzza for the king, but from Cotton's corps of Regulators, two companies marched off the field and returned to their homes. The army decamped at midnight, retraced their steps and crossed the river at Campbelton. About daylight, on the morning of the twenty-first, the army, with the baggage having been landed on the north side, destroyed or sunk the boats, to prevent the pursuit of the enemy, and then resumed its march, sending a party

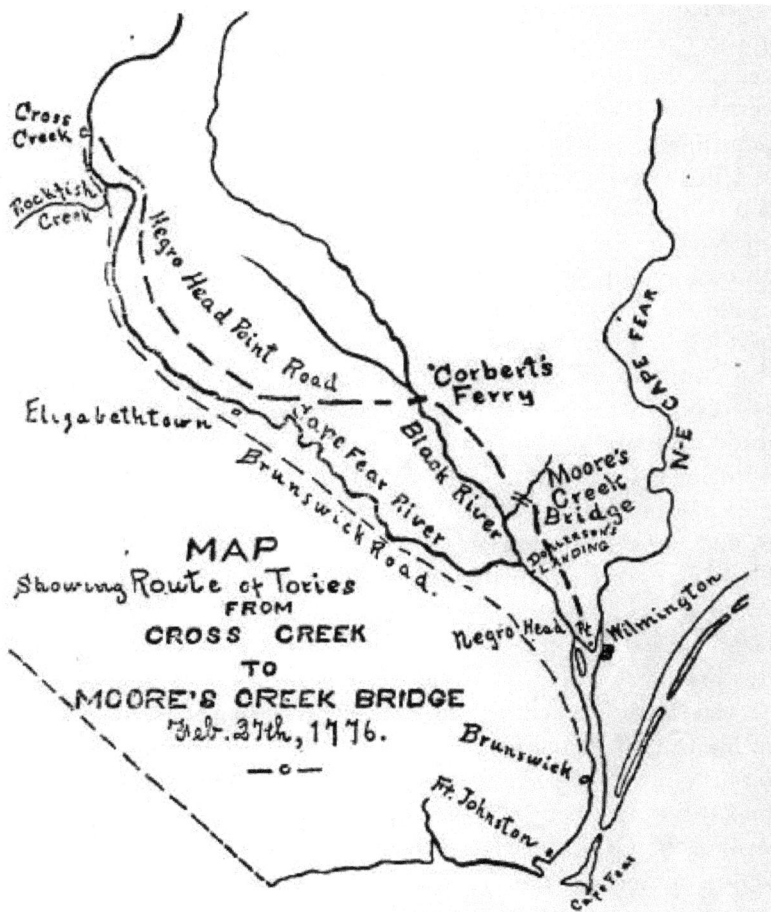

Cross Creek

Rockfish Creek

Negro Head Point Road

Cape Fear River

Elizabethtown

Brunswick Road

Corbert's Ferry

Black River

N·E CAPE FEAR

Moore's Creek Bridge

Dobberson's Landing

MAP

Showing Route of Tories

FROM

CROSS CREEK

TO

MOORE'S CREEK BRIDGE

Feb. 27th, 1776.

—o—

Negro Head

Ft. Wilmington

Brunswick

Ft. Johnston

Cape Fear

fifteen miles in advance to secure the bridge over South River from Bladen into Hanover, pushing with rapid pace over swollen streams, rough hills, and deep morasses, hotly pursued by General Moore.

Perceiving the purpose of the enemy, General Moore instantly put in execution every precaution. He sent off an express to Colonel Caswell directing him to return and take possession of Corbett's Ferry over Black River, for the purpose of harassing the enemy, and impeding its progress. Thackston and Martin were to hold possession of Cross Creek and prevent a retreat in that direction, and Lillington and Ashe were ordered to make a forced march, and, if possible, reinforce Colonel Caswell, and if that could not be done, then to take possession of the Widow Moore's Creek Bridge, on the same road but nearer Wilmington. Apprehending that the enemy might attempt to pass through Duplin, pursuing a route to the eastward, the bridges of that county were in part destroyed, Colonel Cray holding back Salter's company for that purpose, and all the inhabitants held themselves ready to demolish the remainder if necessary to obstruct the march of the loyalists.

At Wilmington, Colonel Purviance prepared to arrest the boats should the enemy descend the river, and with this intent threw a boom across the stream at Mount Misery, four miles above the town, and there stationed one hundred and twenty men, while another detachment held the pass at Heron's Bridge, ten miles out on the northeast branch.

Having dispatched his orders, General Moore, with the remainder of his army, hastened to Elizabethtown, hoping to strike MacDonald on his route to Corbett's Ferry, or else to fall on his rear and surround him at the river before he could cross. On the twenty-fourth, Moore crossed the Cape Fear; but having learned that Colonel Caswell was almost entirely out of provisions, he was compelled to wait there until the evening of the next day for a supply. Here he received a dispatch from Colonel Caswell informing him that the enemy had raised a flat, which had been sunk, about five miles above him, and had made a bridge by which the whole army had passed over. On receiving this intelligence. General Moore moved down the river in boats to Dollerson's Landing, about sixty miles, and thence to Moore's Creek, ten miles from the landing. On the twenty-sixth he arrived at Dollerson's in the afternoon.

Caswell, realising the purpose of the enemy, changed his own course in order to intercept the march. On the twenty-third. General MacDonald thought to outwit him, and arraying the Highlanders in order of battle, with eighty able-bodied men, armed with broadswords, forming the centre of the army; but Caswell, being posted at Corbett's Ferry, could not be reached for want of boats. Again the royalists were in extreme danger, but at a point six miles higher up the Black River they succeeded in crossing in a broad, shallow boat, while MacLean and Fraser were left with a few men, and a drum and fife, to amuse Caswell.

Lillington, on the twenty-fifth, took possession of Widow Moore's Creek Bridge; and on the next day Caswell reached the west side, threw up a slight embankment, and destroyed a part of the bridge. A royalist, who had been sent into his camp under pretext of summoning him to return to his allegiance, brought back the information that Caswell had halted on the same side of the river as themselves, and could be assaulted to advantage. Caswell was both a good woodsman and a man of superior ability, and believing that he had misled the enemy, marched his column to the east side of the stream, removed the planks from the bridge, greased the sleepers with soft soap and tallow, and then placed his men behind trees and such embankments as could be thrown up during the night.

The force amounted to a thousand men, consisting of the Newbern minute-men, the militia of Craven, Dobbs, Johnston, and Wake counties, besides the detachment under Lillington. The men of the Neuse region, their officers wearing silver crescents upon their hats, inscribed with the words, "Liberty or Death," were in front. The situation of the Highlanders was again perilous, for while facing this army, Moore, with his regulars, was close upon their rear.

CHAPTER 8

Battle of Widow Moore's Creek Bridge

The Highland Army was in a position where it could neither advance nor retreat. General MacDonald had proved himself fertile in resources; but it was now doomed to be deprived of his guiding hand, and those left to direct the army were not equal to the emergencies. The general was taken very ill and confined to his bed, and had been left at a house some eight miles from the scene of action, and this calamity was the precursor of a still heavier one about to fall like a thunderbolt. The Highlanders had been outmanoeuvred, and the patriots had gained an advantageous position, forcing the enemy either to fight or else to take a course which would bring on them the imputation of cowardice and disconcert their plans.

On the evening before the battle a council of war was held, presumably in the presence of General MacDonald, the main object of which was to decide the question whether they should force their way through their adversaries, or determine some other movement. All the old and experienced officers, among whom was Colonel Donald MacLeod, then in command, both by priority of rank and common consent, were strongly opposed to battle, contending that the difficulty and danger of forcing their way in the face of an enemy, two-thirds their number, so strongly posted, defended by their entrenchments, mounted with two pieces of artillery and protected in front by a stream that was impassable except by a narrow bridge, which could be raked by their guns, were too great to be attempted.

Besides, on good authority, it had been learned that by making a detour of only a few miles, the stream could be crossed where they could fight on equal grounds. These considerations, so sound and appealing to military science, were sneered at by others, and especially the young, self-conceited, and hot-headed MacLean, adventurous, spirited, self-willed, emphatically demanded courageous action.

"Well," exclaimed MacLeod, as he closed the council, "at dawn tomorrow we will prove who is the coward."

Colonel MacLeod determined upon an early attack, and at one o'clock on the morning of the twenty-seventh, began his march, but owing to the time lost in passing an intervening morass, it was within an hour of daylight when they reached the west bank of the creek. Seventy men were selected, of the stoutest and most resolute in the army, and formed into a company under the command of Captain John Campbell, who were to have the post of greatest danger. They were to rush over the bridge in front of the army and storm the works, sword in hand. The fate of this company was the most important, for on it depended the issue of battle.

The Highlanders advanced through the open pine woods on a slope of descending ground, their officers well dressed in gay regimentals, banners and plumes waving in the breeze, and all marching in good order but with quick step to the sound of their pibrochs, while the thrilling notes of the bugle were heard in the distance, making a formidable appearance. Without resistance they entered the ground; but seeing Caswell's forces on the opposite bank, they reduced their columns and formed the line of battle in the woods. Their rallying cry was "King George and broadswords," and the signal of attack was three cheers, the drum to beat, and the pipes to play.

While it was still dark MacLeod, accompanied by Captain John Campbell on his right, with a party of about forty of the swordsmen, advanced and at the bridge was challenged by one of the sentinels asking, "Who goes there?"

He answered, "A friend."

"A friend of whom?"

"To the king."

Upon this the sentinels bowed their faces down to the ground. MacLeod, thinking they might be some of his own command who had crossed the bridge, challenged them in Gaelic, but receiving no reply, fired his own piece, and ordered his party to fire also. All that remained of the bridge were the two pine sleepers, stripped of their bark and well-greased.

The night before the battle. Colonel Caswell received information of the contemplated attack. This put him on his guard, and he made his arrangements accordingly. Lillington's men were drawn up across the peninsula, and lay on their arms all night. One of the pieces of artillery, known among the soldiers as "Mother Covington," a special favourite of the men, was placed in a position to command the bridge.

Colonel MacLeod and Captain Campbell rushed upon the sleepers of the bridge and succeeded in getting over. The Highlanders that followed had difficulty in keeping on the sleepers, some supporting themselves by thrusting their swords into the logs, and others falling into the muddy stream below. Lillington gave the command to fire, and the musketry swept the bridge. At last "Mother Covington" let go, with terrible effect. MacLeod was mortally wounded, but was seen to rise repeatedly from the ground, waving his sword and encouraging his men to come on, until twenty-six balls had penetrated his body. Campbell was shot dead, and at the same moment a party of militia under Lieutenant Ezekiel Slocum, who had forded the creek and penetrated a swamp on its western bank, fell suddenly upon the rear of the royalists. The loss of their leader, and the unexpected attack upon the rear, threw them into confusion, when all broke and fled.

There were probably twenty who got over the bridge, but all were killed or wounded, all of whom belonged to Campbell's company. Among them were Duncan MacRae, William Stewart, Kenneth Murchison, Laughlin Bethune, Murdoch MacRae, Alexander Campbell, and John MacArthur, of whom the three last were taken to Wilmington the next morning, and all died of their wounds within a week. There was among them a man from Cross Creek, by the name of Campbell, called in Gaelic "Far-earst," who by a desperate kind of valour, rushed over the bridge, but had hardly set his foot on the ground when his body was literally riddled by the rifle balls and he fell dead on the spot. MacLean survived his wound and in after life became sedate and saddened over the fate of MacLeod.

The Highlanders lost about seventy killed and wounded, while the patriots had none killed and two wounded, one of whom recovered. The victory was complete, decisive, and lasting, for the power of the Highlanders was completely broken. There fell into the hands of the Americans eight hundred and fifty prisoners, fifteen hundred rifles, all of them excellent pieces, three hundred and fifty guns and shot-bags, two hundred and fifty swords and dirks, two medicine chests, fresh from England, one of which was valued at £300 sterling, thirteen wagons with horses, which proved of great value to the slender supplies of the provincial forces. Besides all this, there was found secreted in a stable at Cross Creek, a box of guineas amounting to $75,000.

Some of the Highlanders escaped from the field of carnage by breaking down their wagons and riding away, three upon a horse. Many of those taken confessed they were forced and persuaded against their inclinations into the service. All the soldiers taken were disarmed and ordered to return to their homes immediately.

The American officers fully realized the importance of capturing all the leaders, for then the Highlanders would remain inactive in their homes. Hence, various companies were sent out to scour the country and apprehend everyone who held rank in the army. On the following day General Donald MacDonald was taken prisoner. He was sitting on a stump and as his captors came up, he waved his commission, perhaps for the reason of being identified and humanely treated. There is a tradition that some of his soldiers surrounded his tent, and in desperation fought in his defence until driven off. Nearly all the chief men were taken the same day, including Allen MacDonald of Kingsburgh, and his son, Alexander.

It is possible that this account may fall to some who are descended from one or more of the prisoners, and, to others related to the victors; hence the completeness of this victory may be seen by giving a partial list of the prisoners, taken from a report of the committee of the Provincial Congress, April 20 and May 10, on the guilt of the Highland and Regulator officers then confined in the jail of Halifax. The prisoners were divided into four classes, namely:

First. Prisoners who had served in Congress.
Second. Prisoners who had signed Tests or Associations.
Third. Prisoners who had been in arms without such circumstances.
Fourth. Prisoners under suspicious circumstances.
The Highlanders coming under these various designations are given in the following order:
Farquhard Campbell, Cumberland county.
Alexander McKay, capt. of thirty-eight men, Cumberland county.
Alexander MacDonald (Condrach), Major of a regiment.
Alexander Morrison, Captain of a company of thirty-five men.
Alexander McDonald, son of Kingsborough, a volunteer, Anson county.
James McDonald, Captain of a company of twenty-five men.

Alexander McLeod, Captain of a company of thirty-two men.

John MacDonald, Captain of a company of forty men.

Alexander McLeod, Captain of a company of sixteen men.

Murdoch McAskell, Captain of a company of thirty-four men.

Alexander McLeod, Captain of a company of sixteen men.

Angus McDonald, Captain of a company of thirty men.

Neill McArthur, Freeholder of Cross Creek, Captain of a company of fifty-five men.

Francis Frazier, Adjutant to General McDonald's Army.

John McLeod, of Cumberland county, Captain of a company of thirty-five men.

John McKinzie, of Cumberland county. Captain of a company of forty-three men.

Kennith MacDonald, *aid-de-camp* to General MacDonald.

Murdoch McLeod, of Anson county. Surgeon to General MacDonald's Army.

Donald McLeod, of Anson county, lieutenant in Captain Morrison's company.

Norman McLeod, of Anson county, ensign in James McDonald's company.

John McLeod, of Anson county, lieutenant in James McDonald's company.

Laughlin MacKinnon, freeholder in Cumberland county, Lieutenant in Col. Rutherford's corps.

James Munroe, freeholder in Cumberland county. Lieutenant in Captain McRey's company.

Donald Morrison, Ensign to Captain Morrison's company.

John McLeod, Ensign to Capt. Morrison's company.

Archibald McEachern, Bladen county. Lieutenant to Capt. McArthur's company.

Rory McKinnon, freeholder, Anson county, volunteer.

Donald McLeod, freeholder, Cumberland county, Master to two regiments, General McDonald's Army.

Donald Stuart, Quarter Master to Col. Rutherford's Regiment.

Allen MacDonald, of Kingsborough, freeholder of Anson county. Col. of Regiment.

Duncan St. Clair.

Daniel McDaniel, Lieutenant to Seymore York's company.

Alexander McRaw, freeholder, Anson county, Capt. of a company of forty-seven men.

Kenneth Stuart, Lieutenant, Capt. Stuart's company.

Collin McIver, Lieutenant, Capt. Leggate's company.

Alexander MacLaine, Commissary to General MacDonald's Army.

Angus Campbell, Captain of a company of thirty men.

Alexander Stuart, Captain of a company of thirty men.

Hugh McDonald, Anson county, volunteer.

John McDonald, common soldier.

Daniel Cameron, common soldier.

Daniel McLean, freeholder, Cumberland county, Lieutenant to Angus Campbell's company.

Malcolm McNeill, recruiting agent for General MacDonald's Army, accused of using compulsion.

Some of the prisoners were discharged soon after their arrest, by signing a proper oath not to bear arms against the United States.

Most of the prominent characters among both the Highlanders and Regulators, some of whom had not been in the battle, but considered to be dangerous to the best interests of the province, were made prisoners and remanded for trial. Among these were Thomas Rutherford and Farquhard Campbell, men of intelligence, wealth, and influence. Both were members of the first convention of August 25, 1774; members of the second convention, signed the articles of Association, April 3, 1775; members of the first Congress which met in August, 1775.

Their votes were in unison with the rest, but all the time kept up a good understanding with the royalists. For a day or two before the battle at Moore's Creek, Campbell was with General MacDonald giving information and advice, and the next day with Caswell for the same purpose, and was actually present with him during the engagement, making suggestions and pretending a deep interest in the fortunes of the day.

There are still many interesting incidents detailed concerning the flight of some who took part in the battle. There were others which taught the Americans to be constantly on their guard. Among those narrated is the action of Colonel Reid and Captain Cunningham, who, with a party of fourteen, after the battle, surprised a company of provincials at Cross Creek, disarmed them and then made their way to Fort Johnson.

177

CHAPTER 9

Results of the Battle

It is the design not to enter into a free discussion of the important results accruing from the defeat of the Highlanders at Moore's Creek, nor follow up details of acts, however interesting they may be. There are certain historical matters which should be adverted to. As this battle was the first fought on North Carolina soil during the American Revolution, it would have results that might be far-reaching in their consequences.

On the Americans the victory had a most potent effect. It animated them with hope, established confidence, increased valour, and kindled the flames of patriotism. An enthusiastic patriot, writing under date of March 10, 1776, says:

> It is inconceivable to imagine what joy this event has diffused through this province; the importance of which is heightened by Clinton and Lord William Campbell's being now in Cape Fear. How amazingly mortified must they prove in finding that this weak, poor, and insignificant Carolina, in less than fifteen days, could turn out more than ten thousand independent gentlemen volunteers, and within that time pursue them to the very scene of action. Since I was born I never heard so universal an ardour for fighting prevail and so perfect a union among all classes of men.

True to their profession, the leaders of the patriots determined to treat the Highlanders in general with the utmost consideration. This fact Stedman clearly recognises, for he records that Colonel Moore and Colonel Caswell "behaved with great leniency and moderation towards the loyalists while they continued in power."

The defeat of this army disconcerted the plans of Governor Martin, but he adhered to the idea that if a considerable force should penetrate into the interior, thousands of loyalists would flock to the royal standard. Even Cornwallis showed the same idea as late as 1781, when he marched his army into Cross Creek. The loyalists, though disheartened, generally remained faithful to the crown, but disarmed and deprived of their leaders, the Highlanders had not the heart again to enter the army. They had also taken a parole which nearly all kept inviolate.

During the whole course of the war, the Highlanders were regarded with suspicion, probably caused by unruly spirits among them. The Americans did not rest matters simply by confining the officers, but every precaution was taken to overcome them, not only by their parole, but also by armed force, for a militia company at once was stationed at Cross Creek until November 21. On July 28, 1777, it was reported that the royalists were in motion, which aroused the Americans to arms and a vigilant watch was kept over those at Cross Creek. So, also, the Highlanders were kept in alarm. In June, 1776, it was reported among them that a company of light horse was coming into the settlement, and everyone thought he was the man wanted, and hence all hurried to the swamps and other fastnesses in the forest.

From the poor Highland women, who had lost father, husband, brothers in battle, or whose menfolk were imprisoned in the jail at Halifax there went up such a wail of distress as to cause the Provincial Congress to put forth a proclamation, ordered to be printed into the "Erse tongue," in which it was declared that they "warred not with those helpless females, but sympathized with them in their sorrow," and recommended them to the "bounty of those who had aught to spare from their necessities."

The district in which the Highlanders were settled was in a tumult for some time after the battle at Moore's Creek. Colonel Caswell marched through the district, but allowed no violence, trying in all cases to be just. But there were independent parties who committed outrages, of which the legal officers were guiltless. There was much suffering caused by the lawless. These inhuman acts were deplored by all the better class, but owing to the disordered state of society, such things were often beyond their control. Then the people were aggravated by the acts of British agents who kept up the turmoil. Hector MacNeill and Archibald Douglas, of the British army, came into the district and tried to exert an influence over the people, declaring the British had money to any amount; that they would conquer the country, and that the Scotch would be handsomely rewarded if found on the king's side. Again the Highlanders began to embody, and from that time until the close of the war, the country presented a terrible scene of bloodshed, devastation, and ruin.

From the opening to the close of the Revolution, there were Highlanders in North Carolina enrolled in both the contending forces. Those on the British side were mostly recent emigrants, the bulk of whom were not familiar with the English language. Some, however, were with the patriots, and fought with Marion and other commanders. Those Highlanders belonging to earlier emigrations were principally loyal to their adopted country. The contentions of the same race, each party striving for mastery would naturally provoke the most severe animosities.

The act of the insurgents of 1776 enrolled in General MacDonald's army is sometimes called "The Insurrection of the MacDonalds." During and after the war these people, to a great number, withdrew from the State, some returning to Scotland, and others settled in Nova Scotia.

It will not be necessary, in this connection, to follow the history of the officers imprisoned in Halifax jail. I have already done that in my *Scotch Highlanders in America*. However, we must present the final struggles of Allen and Flora MacDonald.

With other captured officers, Allen was closely confined in the jail at Halifax. On April 11, 1776, the North Carolina Provincial Congress resolved that Allen be admitted to his parole; that he should not go without the limits of the town of Halifax; that he should not correspond with any person who is inimical to American interests ; that he shall not convey intelligence to such person ; that he will take no plans or drafts while on parole, and that every day between the hours of ten and twelve o'clock he shall report to the officer of the guard.

According to a letter dated April 22, 1776, General Donald MacDonald, Colonel Allen MacDonald of Kingsburgh, his son, Alexander, Major Alexander MacDonald, besides fifteen captains, one lieutenant, and five minor officers, including the chaplain, Rev. John Bethune, all of the Highland Army, were sent prisoners to Philadelphia.

On the way from North Carolina to Philadelphia, while resting at Petersburg, May 2, 1776, Kingsburgh wrote the following letter:

Sir: Your kind favour I had by Mr. Ugin (?), with the Virginian money enclosed, which shall be paid if ever I return, with thanks; if not, I shall take to order payment. Colonel Eliot who came here to receive the prisoners confined the general and me under a guard and sentries to a room; this he imputes to the Congress of North Carolina not letting Brigadier Lewes (who commands at Williamsburg) know of our being on parole by your permission when at Halifax. If any opportunity afford, it would add to our happiness to write something to the above purpose to some of the Congress here with directions (if such can be done) to forward said orders after us. I have also been depressed of the horse I held, and hath little chance of getting another. To walk on foot is what I never can do the length of Philadelphia. What you can do in the above different affairs will be adding to your former favours. Hoping you will pardon freedom, wrote in a hurry. I am with real esteem and respect, Honourable Sir, your very obedient servt.

Allen MacDonald.

On June 28, Kingsburgh was permitted, after signing a parole and word of honour, to go to Reading, in Berks County, Pennsylvania. At the same time the Committee of Safety

Resolved, That such prisoners from North Carolina as choose, may be permitted to write to their friends there; such letters to be inspected by this Committee, and the jailer is to take care that all the paper delivered in to the prisoners be used in such letters, or returned him.

The action of the Committee of Safety was approved by the Continental Congress, which, on July 9, 1776:

Resolved, That the committee of safety of Pennsylvania release Allan McDonald, of Kingsborough, a prisoner in the gaol of Philadelphia, on his parole, and that, upon his signing his parole, he be treated agreeable to former resolutions of Congress.

His son was ordered released by Congress on the fifteenth by the following resolution:

Resolved, That Alexander McDonald, son of Captain McDonald, be liberated on his parole, and allowed to reside with his father.

On September 25, the Continental Congress received a report from the Committee on the Treasury, in which it is stated that:

There is due to Colonel Allen McDonald of Kingsborough, and his son, Alexander McDonald, for their allowance of two dollars per week for 21 weeks, and for their servants' allowance, 21 weeks, at one dollar per week, settled to the 17th September, 105 dollars.

The time when Allen MacDonald was removed from Philadelphia to Reading, I have not been able to determine. He was removed to the latter place, where were confined Allen MacDonald, St., Allen MacDonald, Jr., Alexander MacDonald, Rennel MacDonald, and Archibald MacDonald, hostages from the Mohawk settlement, sent there by General Philip Schuyler.

On April 10, 1777. Congress received the following petition from Allen MacDonald:

> The petition of Capt: Allen McDonald of Kingsburgh, to John Hancock Esquire, in Congress.—Humbly sheweth—
> That whereas your petitioner and son, are now nigh fourteen months prisoners of war, and were above four months of those, in close confinement, removed from one gaol, to another, and different places of confinement, in North Carolina Virginia, and Maryland, till they arrived in Philadelphia, from there—they were admitted on parole, to reside at Riading, in the County of Berks, where they now are. From whence I am hopefull, it will be certified by His Excellency General Mifflin, Commanding Officer there and the County Committee, that they kept closs to their parole, without giving the smalest offence to any person whatever—
> Your petitioner begs leave further to observe, that provision—drink, lodging, cloathing, and in short everything, is so extravagantly high priced, that prisoners must be in a very miserable state, two dollars, the common allowance pr. week, being of greater service, ten months before now, than six this day—From the above different circumstances; Your petitioner expects, you will exchange him, and son for officers of the like denomination, or order them to New York on parole, till duly exchanged.—And in complying with either of the above requests; you will very much relieve and oblige—
> Sir—Your very Humble and Obedient Servant.
>   Allen McDonald.
> Riading, Aprile 5th, 1777.

Petitioner hath not received even the small allowance of two dollars (*word omitted*)-eek, for himself. Son and servant, from the 30th December last—(*word torn off*) received what was due till then, from his Excellency General Mifflin.

Endorsement: Petition. Capt. Allen McDonald of Kingsburgh— Prisoner on parole in Riading.—

10 April, 1777, No. 8. Petition of Allen McDonnel
     read 10 April 1777
     referred to board of war

On June 10, 1777, the following was offered in Congress:

That General Washington be directed to propose an exchange of Lt. Colonel Allan McDonald and Lt. Alexander McDonald for such officers of equal Rank as are entitled to a priority of Exchange.

On July 22, 1777, Congress received the following from "Alexander (Allen) McDonald of Kingsborrow":

Sir: Some time passd, I petitioned Congress through your hands, in regard to my being exchanged, with my son; which. His Excelency General Mifflin, was so good, as deliver you; Thereafter the chairman of the committee here, James Reid Esqr: wrott to some of the members of Congress, that the voice of the people had made joice of Lt. Colonel Lutes (who was permited to come home on parole by His Excelency Sir William Howe) as their Colonell, and represented me as the fittest person to be exchanged for him, through my good behaviour and strict attention, with my son, to our parole (as they were pleased to term it) since we came here—No return being made to this. The whole officers of the 4th: Battalion of Pensylvania Militia in a body signed a petition to Congress, praying Colonell Lutes being released from the secret tyes of his parole, by exchanging him for me, for the above reasons. What, success this last petition had, I have not yet learned, tho I fear, it shaired the same fate with the former—Now Sir, permit me to say; when you'll know, the dispersed, and distress't state of my family, you will, at least sympathize with me, and pity my oppressed mind. I am here with one of my sons seventeen months a prisoner— My wife is in North Carolina 700 miles from me in a very sickly tender state of health, with a younger son, a daughter, and four grandchildren—Two sons in our service of whom, I heared little or nothing, since one of them had been wounded in the Battle of Bunkers hill—And two in Britain, of whom I heared no accounts since I left it—Them in Carolina I can be of no service to in my present state, but were I exchanged, I would be of service to the rest if in life. If not, with the assistance of the Almighty my mind wou'd be fixed.

Now Sir, let me further tell you, I am a captain in the regular service, and my son a lieutenant, I rank as Lieut. Colonel of Militia in North Carolina; in this station I was made prisoner, and I am convinced Sir William Howe will exchange me in either of those ranks—if not—I hereby binde my honour, my character, and even my life, I, and my son will returne—if Colonell Lutes is not to be exchanged, fix on whome you please of equal rank, and a lieut: for my son; let me bring their names to General Howe and if they are not sent, we will upon honour, and conscience, return to our former parole—Here is Capt. Graydon of your regular service come home with some other gentlemen on parole. Could not he be exchanged for me, and some lieut: you please for my son—Hopeing you'll pardon the anguish of an uneasy mind, and contribute to its relief, which is but charity—I am with respect Sir—

> Your very humble—
> and obedrent servant—
> Allen McDonald of Kingsborrow

Riading July 18th 1777
To—
Address: The Honble. John Hancock President—
    of the Continental Congress—
    Philadelphia—
Endorsement: Letter from Alex. McDonald
    of Kingsborrow 18 July 1777
    read 22
    referred to the board of war
    reported upon

On August 7, 1777, Congress received a report from the Auditor General, in which he states that:

There is due to Allan McDonald, his son and servant, for their allowance as prisoners, from the 18 September, 1776, to the 5

August, 1777, being 46 weeks, the sum of 230 dollars."

Attempts were made to exchange the Highland prisoners on the part of General Washington, and others in authority, but as the captives were so unfortunate as to have no one to intercede for them among those at British headquarters, on August 21, 1777, Congress, in passing upon a report from the Board of War:

> Resolved, That Allan McDonald, of Kingsborough, North Carolina, a captain in the British regular service, be permitted to go into New York to negotiate an exchange for himself and his son, a lieutenant in the same service; he to give his parole not to convey to the enemy or bring back any intelligence whatever of a political nature, and to return in a certain time to be fixed by his parole or when called for, on behalf of the United States.

Kingsburgh proceeded to New York, and during the month of November succeeded in effecting his exchange, and was soon placed in command of a company of provincials.

From the *Letter-Book of Captain Alexander MacDonald of the Royal Highland Emigrants* we catch glimpses of Kingsburgh and his sons, with letters directed to him, here given in full, as they are of interest to all who may desire to know of Flora MacDonald's family:

> Halifax (N. S.) 18 Oct., 1777.
> Dear Cousin: I am extremely happy to hear that you and your son were safe at New York. I hope to have the further pleasure of seeing you both soon here in case you should have occasion or be at a loss for want of money I send you enclosed the state of your account from which you can see how much you may venture to draw for. If Major Donald McDonald (Brigadier-General Donald MacDonald, who commanded in North Carolina), is there yet pray give him my kind compliments. I should have wrote him long before now if I did not think he had gone to England when General McLean left that place.
> I have seen a pretty lad here a son of his lieut. of marines. You may tell him he was very well and expected soon to be in England. I dare say Ronald will write to you by this opportunity they are very happy at the thoughts of seeing you soon and for God's sake don't stay long come to us before the winter sets in and bring all the fine fellows you possibly can get along with you but dont venture in anything less than a frigate. Give

185

my kind compliments to Sandy though a stranger and am dear cousin.

Yours Sincerely.

Halifax, 31st Decr, 1777.

Dear Cousin: It is with sincere pleasure and satisfaction I received yours of the 30th November *ultimo*. You have surely wrote it in the morning early else St. Andrew would have prevented the pleasure of my receiving a letter from you of that date and nothing can give me greater pleasure than to hear of you and your son being safe out of the hands of the rebels. I am also happy to hear of Mrs. Macdonald's welfare and her spirited behaviour when brought before the committee of rascals in North Carolina.

I don't doubt but she and the other gentlewomen there will be sorely oppressed by the savage cruelty of those wretches who at present has the upper hand of them though they may sorely repent it before this war is at an end.

I had rather you was here at the head of your own company in our regiment than commanding a company of Provincials which as we have a great many enemys may be made a handle of to hinder our establishment. Major Small who goes by this opportunity will talk to you more fully on this subject. The rank of the officers of this regiment is already settled by Major Small and the rest of the officers present upon the spot. How far the commission you speak of will avail you I do not know but I think Sandy McLeod B :M: did try to get rank from it when Frazier's regiment was raised last war but I believe was refused however you'll be in the right to try it if ever the regiment be established if not it will not be worth your trouble.

I have all your subsistance from the date of your commission to the 24th Feby, 1778, also your arrears and what baggage and fforage money has been allowed since as the inclosed abstracts will show, your son Sandys, as well as your own for which sums or whate part of them you plese you and Sandy may draw if you have not drawn on me allready to the amount of the ballances in yours favours. You see I have payed some money on your account to Capt. Murdock McLean but should it not be agreeable to you I have it still in my power to recharge the same to Capt. McLaine, as he has a chance to see you soon you will settle matters and let me know.

I would not advise you to venture here but in a man of warr and I assure you I think this part of British America the happiest spot in it at present and would be very hapie to see you and all the othere officers of our corps here with all cliver ffellows of recruits you can bring with you—we want about 85 to compleat but we expect a great manney from Newfoundland and from your endeavours—I hope Major Small will sende Capt. Alexander Campbell to joine his company or oblidge him to quitt, which I darr saie he will do for a triffle and I hope in that case you will secure it for Sandy being the 2nd oldest lieutt. If there is no certainty of our establishment I am convinced Campbell will rathere give up the company for nothing rather than be obliged to joine at lest would be glad to take one or two hundered pounds for it I mean the company because (indeed) I would not think safe to pay above one years purchass for it though I would be sory that anybody eles should purchass overy Sandys head.

As your son Ranald is going will be the bearer of this I need not trouble you with any news to tell the truth there are none, only he will give you a description of the place he is a fine young ffellow and will make an excellent officer if he lieves— You tell me you have contracted a great deall of debt, I darr saie you must have lieved expensive but it is high time now my dear Allan to study oeconomy your 3 oldest sons are provided for espetialy if this regiment will established therefore has no right to expect any more assistance from you, if you was worth ten thousand a year except when a purchase came in their way. I darr saie you and your volhmteers make a formidable figure in the dress you have described to me which I perfectly understand all but the cuteikins which I take to be half boots or geatters.

I cannot give you the lest accot of poor Normand Talisker some people told me he and his wife went home what to do there God only knows I don't know that I felt more concerned for a man in my life than I have for him curse the grogg at lest too much of it. I'm hapy to hear poor John McLean and Peggy are unmollested, I wish they may continue so. Pray for Godsake is it possible to gett Mrs. McDonald and the othere poor women from N. Carolina—I thought my worthy ffriende Major Donald McDonald had gone to England long ago if this findes him with you pray offer him my most humble respects.

Bring with you or sende to us some syder and aples of the best sort if they can be gote if you can go with safety to Staten Island I wish you would be so good as to sende or order to be sent some negro chielderen that are at my house as their mothere is dead, unless you finde matters are like to be sattled in which case I would let them stay where they are I again wish we were alltogethere as the more we are in one place the more respectable our appearance wishing you and all ffriends the complments of the season and with Mrs. McDonald's and my kinde wishes for everything that can make you hapy and ever I am with sincerity and truth dear cousin

    Yours affectionatly

                                                  A. M. D.

The third letter is dated

                            Halifax, 12th January, 1778.

Dear Cousin: Since my last of the 31st of December *ultimo* which will be delivered to you by your son Ronald who from some hints I received is going there not only with anxiety to see you but with some other views to get you to lay out the little money you have in my hands in purchasing a higher commission for himself or Charles a manuvre I would highly approve of if you could afford it, but I have already given a hint upon this head and I again tell you that I think your three sons extremely well provided for consigering their age especially is this regiment be established as I hope it is by this time.

Ronald is already in a very good corps and pretty far advanced and probably may have a chance for a company before this work is at an end. Charles is a fine young fellow for whom I have the sincerest regard but the income of a general officer would be rather small for him, if he could get it, he is very sensible and very clever when sober but rather unhappy when he is any ways disguised in liquor but your presence here might be the means of altering him and putting a stop to it.

These circumstances are as galling to me to relate as they can possibly be to you to hear them but I think it my duty from the sincerest friendship to acquaint you with them. Were so near relations indifferent to me I might laugh as others do and pass it over in silence. I beg You would not let Ronald or Charles know any part of this intelligence but with the power and authority of a parent command Ronald at his peril to tell you the truth of all he knows concerning Charles and his behaviour.

I have nothing earthly to lay to his charge but what the effects of liquor is the cause of and a propensity to extravagance would I wish to God he was cured of as no man has a right to spend more than his income and not even that it being much more honourable for a young officer to have a guinea in his pocket to lend to his comrade than to be obliged to borrow one from him and I beg you would keep a tight hand and learn them to live upon their pay especially as you have other things to do with your money and other people to provide for. In short I wish you was here for several good reasons. This will be delivered you by your old acquaintance Capt. Murdock McLean, a sensible facetious clever honest worthy fellow. As its supposed you are acquainted with all the Scotch folks in New York you will no doubt introduce Capt. McLean to them all.

Wishing you a speedy and safe arrival here with great good news from the southward I remain dear cousin

Yours sincerely.

The last letter is dated

> Halifax, 19th Feby, 1778.

The above is a copy which I intended to send by Capt. Murdock McLane but he departed in such a hurry that I could not get it finished. Since which time I have nothing new to tell you only the departure of our worthy major who left us the 27th of January and hope is now safe in London where he will insist upon the fate of our regiment before he leaves it. So it is to be hoped that two months will satisfy our anxiety and curiosity.

I sent my two eldest boys along with him to the care of William Macdonald of Edinburgh and to be sent to the Highlands for one or two years if he approves of it.

I furnished your son Ronald with five half *joannis* which I placed to your account as he expected to get an order from you for that purpose and I was obliged within these few days to accommodate Charles with above £50 sterling he has by the management of your company the 3 contingent which is equal to £27.9 sterling a year and £10 paid him out of your baggage and forrage money by order of Major Small. If all this is not sufficient to support Charles what will other poor subalterns do who has not a farthing but their bare subsistance.

I understand that Charles and Ronald are entirely against your joining the regiment. I dont know what good reason they can have for it but one thing I am sure of it is absolutely necessary that you should be as near them as possible to overawe their conduct and assist them with your good advice and without you clearly see that you can do better for yourself by staying where you are I would earnestly recommend it to you to join the regiment as soon as possible with all the officers and recruits you can possibly bring along with you as well for the above reasons as for the character of the regiment. As the more there are together of us the more respectable appearance we'll make and of course the better chance we'll have to compleat our wishes of establishment.

Bad as this place was always reckoned this certainly the most peaceable corner now in America and if you can by any means obtain a safe conduct for Mrs. Macdonald and Mrs. McLeod you might order them to follow you to this place.

I have no more to add but to assure you that I am dear cousin

Your real friend and honourable servant.

In a letter addressed to Gen. Francis MacLean, dated Halifax, July 5, 1778, Capt. Alexander Mac Donald speaks of a letter that the former had sent by Allen MacDonald, but the last named had not yet arrived. Reference is also made of the cash advanced by Gen. MacLean to Allen MacDonald and his thirty recruits. The last reference to Kingsburgh is in a letter dated Halifax, August 21, 1778, in which is the statement:

If Capt. Murdock McLean or Capt. Allan Macdonald should be there (New York) tell them as I have said before it is very surprising what keeps them there that I will certainly stop their credit from receiving any more money if they dont join the regiment or assign sufficient reasons to the contrary.

Just when Kingsburgh left New York for Halifax, Nova Scotia, I am unable to discover. It is, however, probable, sometime during the autumn of 1778. He joined his regiment, the Eighty-Fourth, or Royal Highland Emigrant Regiment, Second Battalion, taking command of the Eighth Company, his commission dating from June 14, 1775. He was deprived of the rank assigned him by Governor Martin. The Second Battalion was commanded by Major John Small. About the close of 1778, the regiment received establishment. The uniform was the full Highland garb, with purses made of raccoon skins. The officers wore the broadsword and dirk, and the men a half-basket sword. That part remaining in Nova Scotia saw but little service. Allen MacDonald remained with his regiment, without seeing any particular service, until its reduction in 1783, when he returned to Skye, as a captain on half pay. On his arrival at Portree, he was met by Flora, with a numerous party of friends, to welcome him. Immediately he set out for the estate of Kingsburgh, which during his absence in America, had been left open for his return.

As already noted, the son, Alexander, was released from imprisonment at the same time as the father, and the two proceeded together to New York. The next glimpse of Alexander we find him at Fort Edward, Nova Scotia, November 23, 1778. The next, he was put in command of the prize crew on board the *Ville de Paris,* and, together with his brother, Ranald, went down with that vessel, October 5, 1782. How Ranald reached the army I am not informed. It seems reasonable to assume he was not at the Battle of the Widow Moore's Creek Bridge. From MacDonald's *Letter Book,* it appears that Charles received, in 1776, a commission of lieutenant from Major Small, and was warmly recommended by Earl Percy.

MacKenzie, in his *History of the MacDonalds,* states that Flora's son, James, was "a brave officer, who served with distinction in Tarlton's British Legion," but does not mention the part performed by John.

CHAPTER 10

Final Trials of Flora MacDonald

Flora MacDonald was soon aroused to the fact that the battle was disastrous to her and her immediate countrymen, and that her husband, a son, and her son-in-law were incarcerated in the jail at Halifax, North Carolina. Woes rapidly crowded upon her, all of which, in the spirit of a true heroine, she attempted to surmount. She was denied the privilege of visiting her husband and never saw him again in America.

War is the reverse of humanity. Its horrors have been pictured by the ablest pens. It arouses all the baser passions. Fortunately, there are redeeming qualities. There are characters able to rise preeminent. There is no evidence that Flora MacDonald was ever bitter, vindictive, or unforgiving. In short, her character, from any viewpoint, is one to be admired. True, she was instrumental in bringing on the war, but she paid the penalty without a murmur and without a censure. The Battle at Moore's Creek must have struck a knell of woe to her heart. All her sons were in the British service. Her only married daughter, Anne, was settled in a house of her own, and her daughter, Fanny, was still in precarious health from the dregs of a recent fever, and yet too young to sympathize in her mother's distress.

The revolution around her was rapid and changing; plots and intrigues various; alarms constant, and every passing day placed her in a position where her mind hovered between hope and fear. Nor was this all. She was an object of suspicion, and her every movement was noted. Had she not been prominent in the rising of the MacDonalds? Had she not spoken words of encouragement to and exhorted the Highland Army to be brave? Was it not reasonable to conclude that her interest and determination were still the same?

It would be but reasonable to assume that Flora MacDonald should suffer for what she had done, when the war spirit was dominant. True, she was not arrested, nor imprisoned, nor, in person, was she molested. But the purported evidence against her was so great, that she was summoned before the Committee of Safety. True to her character, during the examination she is said to have exhibited a "spirited behavior." She was permitted to return home in peace, but not so to remain, for war produces lawlessness. Irresponsible parties, taking advantage of the unsettled state of affairs, ravished her plantation and pillaged her residence.

As previously noted, her estate was confiscated by the Act of November, 1777, passed by the Provincial Congress at Newbern, when she sought a home on the plantation of old Kenneth Black. If any person was seen in her company it was sufficient evidence that the party was disloyal to the cause of America. Added to all her misery she was called to grieve the loss of a son and a daughter, who died of typhus fever, aged respectively eleven and thirteen, buried at Killiegrey. Their names have not been preserved. In after years the kind-hearted proprietor of Killiegrey, Mr. Gray, fenced in the graves, erected a small monument to mark the spot, and cared for the same up to the breaking out of the Civil War, but now none of the older citizens residing near the place, know anything about the location of the graves.

Mistreatment was perpetrated on her daughters. Caruthers, in his *Revolutionary Incidents*, has preserved an account of the massacre at Piney Bottom, a branch of the Rockfish. Here Colonel Wade, returning home in a peaceable manner, with a few men to guard the families with him, was surprised in the night by a large party of Tories, who shot down five or six and then plundered the camp. Colonel Wade immediately collected about one hundred dragoons. They came into Richmond County, caught Daniel Patterson and whipped him until he gave the names of all he knew who were at Piney Bottom. In Moore County they caught quite a number and put them to death. Some of the party came to old Kenneth Black's house. Both doors being open, the men rode in until it was full of horses, and the family were crowded into the chimney. Mr. Black's family having had the smallpox, two daughters of Flora MacDonald, Mrs. Anne MacLeod and Fanny, came over to see their friends;

> But, to their utter surprise, they found the Whigs there, who took the gold rings from their fingers and the silk handkerchiefs from their necks ; then putting their swords into their bosoms,

split down their silk dresses and, taking them out into the yard, stripped them of all their outer clothing.

In the above account Caruthers has his date wrong, or else the incident confused with another.

Under all the adverse circumstances Flora continued calm, peaceful, and resigned in her demeanour.

Allen MacDonald managed to have a letter delivered to Flora, in which he advised her to return to the Isle of Skye. It was her desire to remain in America, though in distress and her means limited. She decided to comply with her husband's desire, and leave at the earliest opportunity. Owing to the scouts of the patriots it was a difficult matter to leave the country. But, happening to be at a social gathering, she met Captain Eben Ingram, an American officer, to whom she narrated her difficulties. He promised to use his good offices in her behalf, and soon after secured her a passport from Cross Creek to Wilmington. From thence she secured a passage by vessel to Charleston, South Carolina.

It appears to be well established that in order to secure money to defray her expense she sold her silverware. A silver tray, reputed to have been used for that purpose, was preserved in Wilson, North Carolina. Flora possessed a very large and handsome set of silver, probably presented her while a prisoner in London. While in Wilmington, perceiving she had not enough money for her journey, she was induced to part with it. This was purchased by Richard Quince. The waiter, bowl, ladle, and cream pitcher are now owned by Mrs. E. J. Justice, of Greensboro. Several other pieces are owned by Mrs. Brooke Empie, of Wilmington, and still others widely distributed. It would appear that public enterprise would place all in the State museum at Raleigh. As previously noted. Col. James MacQueen contributed largely, and it is more than probable that others rendered financial assistance.

Killiegrey was forcibly wrenched from Flora MacDonald, and long since the residence was destroyed by fire. Upon that home she had built her hopes and there anticipated spending her declining years. Whatever may have been her misfortunes:

Her name is still held in reverence by the people of North Carolina, and especially by those who are descended from the Scotch settlers of the Cape Fear region. The memory of the Tory beauty, so brave-hearted, and yet so gentle and kind, is as fragrant as the pines among which she lived.

In 1779, accompanied by Fanny alone, still in ill health, of all the family, Flora MacDonald left Charleston on board a British vessel. Crossing the Atlantic the Scottish heroine met with another misfortune. The sloop in which she sailed encountered a French war vessel, and a contest ensued. During the engagement Flora refused to go below, but prominently appeared on deck. The courage of the men appearing to fail, she ascended the quarter-deck, during the fiercest of the battle, and encouraged them to more desperate conduct. She was thrown violently down during the affray and her left arm broken, yet she refused to leave her post, and continued to animate the sailors. She never left the deck until after the French had been beaten off. In after years she was accustomed to say that she had fought for both the House of Stewart and the House of Hanover, but had been worsted in the service of each.

On arriving in Scotland Flora immediately repaired to the residence of her brother in Milton, who erected for her a cottage, where she lived until her husband's return. Nothing of a special nature occurred during her sojourn at Milton. She visited her friends and kept up quite a correspondence with her acquaintances. Two of her letters have been preserved, addressed to the lady of Sir Alexander Muir Mackenzie, who had paid great attention to her son, Alexander, when he was a boy.

The first is as follows:

Dunvegan, Skye, 12th July, 1780.

Dear Madam: I arrived in Inverness the third day after parting with you, in good health, and without any accidents, which I always dread. My young squire continued always very obliging and attentive to me. I staid at Inverness for three days. I had the good luck to meet with a female companion from that to Skye. I was the fourth day, with great difficulty, at Raasay, for my hands being so pained with the riding.

I have arrived here a few days ago with my young daughter, who promises to be a stout Highland "Caileag," quite overgrown of her age. Nanny and her family are well. Her husband was not sailed the last account she had from him.

I have the pleasure to inform you, upon my arrival here, that I had two letters from my husband, the latter dated 10th of May. He was then in very good health, and informs me that my son Charles has got the command of a troop of horse in Lord

TOMB OF FLORA MACDONALD

The monument is an Iona Cross of the St. Martin Cross type. When erected it was the tallest of the kind in existence, its height being 28½ feet. A gale blew it down and broke off ten feet of it. The inscription around the bevelled edge of the flat stone is in ornamental letters, as follows: "Flora Macdonald born at Milton, South Uist 1722. Died at Kingsburgh Skye 4th Mar. 1790." It was erected by subscription. There is a memorial window to Flora MacDonald in St. Columba Episcopal Church, Portree, Skye.

Cathcart's regiment; but alas! I have heard nothing since I left you about my son Sandy, which you may be sure, gives me great uneasiness. But I still hope for the best.

By public and private news, I hope we will soon have peace re-established, to our great satisfaction, which, as it's a thing long expected and wished for, will be for the utility of the whole nation, especially to poor me, that has my all engaged. Fond to hear news, and yet afraid to get it.

I wait here till a favourable opportunity for the Long Island shall offer itself. As I am upon all occasions under the greatest obligations to you, should you get a letter from my son Johnie sooner than I would get one from him, you would very much oblige me by dropping in a few lines communicating to me the most material part of this letter.

I hope you and the ladies of your family will accept of my kindest respects, and I ever am, with esteem,

Dear Madam, your affectionate, humble servant.

        Flora Macdonald.

P. S.—Please direct to me, to Mrs. Macdonald, late of Kingsbor-row, South Uist, by Dunvegan.

To Mrs. Mackenzie of Delvine, by Dunkeld.

The second letter reads:

                                Milton, 3rd July, 1782.

Dear Madam: I received your agreeable favour a fortnight ago, and I am happy to find that your health is not worse than when I left you. I return you my most sincere thanks for your being so mindful of me as to send me the agreeable news about Johny's arrival, which relieved me of a great deal of distress, as that was the first accounts I had of him since he sailed. I think, poor man, he has been very lucky for getting into bread so soon after landing. I had a letter from John which, I suppose, came by the same conveyance with yours. I am told by others that it will be in his power now to show his talents, as being in the engineer's department. He speaks freely of the advantages he got in his youth, and the good example showed him, which I hope will keep him from doing anything that is either sinful or shameful.

I received a letter from Captain Macdonald, my husband, dated from Halifax, the 12th Nov. '81. He was then recovering his health, but had been very tender for some time before. My son, Charles, is a captain in the British Legion, and James a lieutenant in the same. They are both in New York. Ranald is captain of Marines, and was with Rodney at the taking of St. Eustati. As for my son Sandy, who was amissing, I had accounts of his being carried to Lisbon, but nothing certain, which I look upon, on the whole, as a hearsay; but the kindness of Providence is still to be looked upon, as I have no reason to complain, as God has been pleased to spare his father and the rest. I am now in my brother's house, on my way to Skye, to attend my daughter, who is to ly-in August. They are all in health at present. As for my health at present, it's tolerable, considering my anxious mind and distress at times.

It gives me a great deal of pleasure to hear such good accounts of young Mr. Mackenzie. No doubt he has a great debt to pay who represents his worthy and amiable uncle. I hope you will be so good as remember me to your female companions. I do not despair of the pleasure of seeing you once more, if peace was restored; and I am, dear Madam, with respect and esteem, your affectionate friend.

Flora Macdonald.

Having rejoined her husband, immediately after the close of the American Revolution, Flora MacDonald again took up her residence at Kingsburgh house, where she continued to reside until her death, which occurred March 5, 1790, having retained till the last vivacity of character and amiableness of disposition, by which she was distinguished during her whole life. She had gone to a friend's house at Peinduin, in her usual health, to pay a friendly visit, and was there taken suddenly ill with an inflammatory complaint which failed to yield to such medical skill as was available. She retained all her faculties to the last, and calmly departed this life in the presence of her husband and two daughters.

Her remains were shrouded in one of the sheets in which Prince Charles had slept at the mansion of Kingsburgh. During all her travels she had never parted with this sheet. She took it with her to North Carolina, and had it in safe keeping when her own person was in danger. At her own request all that was mortal of her was wrapped in it by her sorrowing family. Under shade of night her body was conveyed from Peinduin to Kingsburgh, the coffin being elevated on the shoulders of a party of stalwart youths selected for the purpose.

The funeral cortege had proceeded but a short distance when it encountered a dreadful storm. The night was of inky darkness, save when relieved by the lightning's red glare. The thunder rolled with terrific peals, and the rain fell in torrents. The Hinisdale was swollen from bank to bank. Some proposed to return, but others declared that she whose body they were carrying had never flinched, when alive, from any duty which she had undertaken, neither would they in performing the last rites to her mortal remains. It was agreed to attempt to cross by the strand near the sea beach, which was effected in safety. Having reached Kingsburgh, the body lay in state for nearly a week. When the day of the funeral arrived several thousand consisting of every rank in Skye and the adjacent isles assembled to pay the last tribute of respect. The procession was a mile in length, and started at an early hour for the churchyard of Kilmuir, at the north end of Skye, sixteen miles distant.

Both Flora's marriage and funeral were the most numerously attended of any in the Western Isles, so far as is known. About a dozen pipers of the schools of MacCrimmon and MacArthur, besides those from other quarters, were present and simultaneously played the *Coronach*, the usual melancholy lament for departed greatness.

On September 20, 1795, Allen MacDonald, Seventh of Kingsburgh, departed this life. He is buried by the side of his wife. Flora, who honoured him with her heart, and for forty years lavished on him all the wealth and all the generous impulses of a truly noble and generous nature.

Over the grave of his mother, John erected a marble slab, set in a frustum frame, but it was cracked in unloading it from the vessel, and in that state was set up. Within a few months tourists had chipped and carried every particle away. By public subscription a costly monument, with an appropriate inscription, was prepared. It is in the form of an Iona cross, a solid monolith of Aberdeen granite, twenty-eight feet high. This was placed at the grave, but failed to resist the blasts of the northern winds. It was upset and broken in two. It has been partly restored. In Inverness is a monument to Flora's memory. It faces toward the home she loved so well.

To Allen and Flora MacDonald were born ten children, three of whom died in childhood, but names not given. Charles was a captain in MacQueen's Rangers; married, without issue. Alexander, an officer in the Insurrection of the MacDonalds, afterwards in the naval service;

went down in the *Ville de Paris*, being on board in command of a prize crew. Never married. Ranald, a captain of marines; unmarried; lost on board the *Ville de Paris*. James served with distinction in Tarleton's Legion; married and had issue. John became Lieutenant-Colonel of the Royal Clan Alpine Regiment, and Commandant of the Royal Edinburgh Artillery; married and had issue. Anne married Major Alexander MacLeod, in 1775, and had issue. In 1834 she died and was buried in her mother's grave. Frances, or Fanny, married Lieutenant Donald MacDonald of Cuidrach. Isle of Skye, with issue.

> *Honoured be woman, she beams on our sight,*
> *Graceful and fair, like a being of light.*
> *She scatters around her, wherever she strays,*
> *Roses of bliss on our thorn-covered ways—*
> *Roses of Paradise sent from above.*
> *To be gathered and twined in a garland of love.*

STATUE OF FLORA MACDONALD ON CASTLE HILL, INVERNESS

This monument was erected at the expense of Capt. T. Henderson Mac-Donald, a direct descendant of Flora, at a cost of $5,000. It faces Skye. On the front is the inscription, "Fhad's a dh' fhá sas flur air machair Mairidh clui na h-ainnir chaoimh."

Translation of the Gaelic: "As long as a flower grows in field the fame of the gentle lady shall endure."

"The preserver of Prince Charles Edward will be mentioned in history and if courage and fidelity be virtues, mentioned with honour."—Johnson.

Copy of the Declaration of Miss MacDonald, Apple Cross Bay, July 12th 1746

Miss McDonald, daughter in law of McDonald of Milton in Sky, being, by General Campbell's order, made prisoner for assisting the eldest son (Bonnie Prince Charlie) of the Pretender in his escape from South Uist, and asked to declare the circumstances thereof, says, that about six weeks ago, she left her father in law's house at Armadach in Sky, and went south to see some friends.

Being asked, if she had any invitation from those who persuaded her to do what she afterwards ingaged in for the young pretender or anybody else, before she left Sky; answered in the negative, and says that at the time of her leaving Sky, she did know where the young Pretender was, but only heard he was somewhere on the Long Island: that she stayed at a sheilling (small hut or cottage) of her brother's, on the hills, near Ormaclait the house of Clan Ronald; and that, about the 21 of June, O'Neil, or as they call him Nelson, came to where she stayed, and proposed to her, that as he heard she was going to Sky, that the young Pretender should go with her.

With her in woman's cloathes, as her servant which she agreed to. O Neil then went and fetched the young Pretender who was on the hills not far off, when they settled the manner of their going.

Miss MacDonald says, that after this she went and stayed with Lady Clan Ronald, at her house, three days, communicated the scheme to her, and desired that she would furnish cloathes for the young Pretender, as her own would be too little. During Miss MacDonald's stay at Ormaclait, O'Neil came frequently from the young Pretender to Clan Ronald's House to inform her where he was, what stepps had been taken for their voiage, and at the same time to hasten her to get her affairs in readiness for going off.

Miss MacDonald says, that the 27th past, she, Lady Clan Ronald, her eldest daughter, and one John MacLean, who had by Lady Clan Ronald's order, acted as cook to the Pretender, during his stay on the hills, went to a place called Whea where they expected to meet the young Pretender; but not finding him there, they went on to a place called Roychenish, where they found him, taking with them the women's apparel furnished by Lady Clan Ronald, he was dressed in.

Here they heard of General Campbell's being come to South Uist, and that Captain Fergussone was within a mile of them. When they got this information, they were just going to supper. But then went of very precipitately, and sat up all night at a sheilling called Closchinisch.

Saturday, June 25th: the cutter and wherrier, which attended General Campbell having got from Bernera, near the Harris, through the last side of the Long Island, and passing not far from them, put them again into great fears, least anybody should land there. However, they continued there 'till about 9 at night, when the young Pretender, Miss Mac Donald, one MacAchran, with five men for the boat's crew, imbarked and put to sea, Lady Clan Ronald having provided provisions for the voyage.

The 29 about 11 in the morning they got to Sky near Sir Alexander MacDonald's house. Here Miss MacDonald and MacAchran landed, leaving the young Pretender in the boat, they went to Sir Alexander MacDonald's house; and from thence Miss MacDonald sent for one Donald Mac Donald, who had been in the rebellion, but had delivered up his arms some time ago. She imployed this person to procure a boat to carry the young Pretender to Rasay, after acquainting him with their late voyage and where she had left the young Pretender. Miss MacDonald stayed and dined with Lady Margaret MacDonald, but MacDonald and MacAchran returned to the boat, to inform what was done.

Miss MacDonald being asked why Rasay was pitched upon for the young Pretender to retreat to, she answered that it was in hopes of meeting Rasay himself, with whom he was to consult for his future security.

After dinner, Miss Mac Donald set out for Portree it being resolved that they should lodge there that night; but on the road overtook the young Pretender and MacAnchran of Kingsbury. She told them she must call at Kingsbury's house, and desired they would go there also.

Here, Miss MacDonald was taken sick, and therefore with the other two, was desired to stay all night, which they agreed to. She had a room to herself; But the young Pretender and MacAchran lay in the same room. At this time, he appeared in women's cloathes, his face being partly concealed by a hood or cloak.

Being asked, if while they were at Kingsbury's house, any of the family inquired who the disguised person was; answers, that they did not ask; but that she observed the people of the family whispering as if they suspected him to be some person that desired not to be known and from the servants she found they suspected him to be MacLeod of Bernera, who had been in rebellion. But, being pressed to declare what she knew or believed of Kingsbury's knowledge of his guest, owns, that she believes, he must suspect it was the young Pretender.

The 30th of June, Miss MacDonald set out on horseback from Kingsbury's house for Portree, having first desired the young Pretender might put on his own cloathes somewhere on the road to Portree, as she had observed that the other dress rather made him more suspected. Miss MacDonald got to Portree about 12 at night, where she found Donald MacDonald, who had been sent before to procure a boat then the young Pretender and MacAncran arrived about an hour after. Here he took some refreshment, changed a guinea, paid the reckoning (bill), took his leave of Miss Mac Donald and went out with Donald Mac Donald, but who, after seeing him to the boat returned. She believes he went to Rasay (island between the Isle of Skye and the Scottish mainland), but cannot tell what is become of him since.

www.ingramcontent.com/pod-product-compliance
Lightning Source LLC
Chambersburg PA
CBHW032058080426
42733CB00006B/321